SCANDALOUS GRACE

SCANDALOUS GRACE

JERIS E. BRAGAN

REVIEW AND HERALD PUBLISHING ASSOCIATION

Washington, DC 20039-0555
Hagerstown, MD 21740

Copyright © 1986 by
Review and Herald Publishing Association

This book was
Edited by Gerald Wheeler
Designed by Richard Steadham

Type set: 11/12 Baskerville

Printed in U.S.A.

R and H Cataloging Service

Bragan, Jeris E., 1946-
    Scandalous grace.

    1. Bragan, Jeris E., 1946-   . 2. Seventh-day
Adventists—United States—Biography. 3. Prisoners—
United States—Biography. I. Title.
286.7'32'0924
ISBN 0-8280-0357-2

Foreword

After clearing security, I joined several others on the visitors' bench looking toward a huge set of doors made of steel rods. Suddenly they snapped open with a bang. Through that door walked a tall, heavy-set blond. "Jeris Bragan!" the guard announced. That was my first glimpse of Jeris. A bond of friendship was immediate. That visit was to be the beginning of a change in my life and the thrust of prison ministry for the Tennessee State Prison and the Seventh-day Adventist Church. You'll find details of that change in this book.

Let me tell you about Jeris. His list of acquaintances includes grandmas, Ph.D.s, journalists, ministers, wardens, students, inmates, married couples, little children—each getting his/her share of his concern, interest, and time. No letter goes unanswered. No question is ignored. People are important to him. In my opinion, each is richer for having known him.

Jeris is a mixture of compassion (when he learns of someone's pain, he will share a gem, often from God's Word) and hard-nosed reporting (following a recent riot, he did the unusual and published the facts, naming heroes and villains). As editor of the prison paper, he has the insight to find out the facts and the courage to speak them.

He is a gifted writer who watches for details often missed by many reporters. The prison does not provide an environment for patience and productivity. Yet in spite of nine years of confinement Jeris remains cool, even under fire. This trait gives him the innate ability to give the facts after the storm has passed.

Jeris's life has taken him through some personal experiences that would have destroyed most. He seeks no scapegoats. Instead he chooses to deal with the world in which he lives, grasping every opportunity to "light a candle instead of cursing the darkness."

I am personally acquainted with many of the characters in his story. I have witnessed what God has done to transform their lives. Can there be a more effective witness to the reality of God and work of the Holy Spirit?

W. C. Arnold
Executive Secretary and Treasurer
Adventist-Laymen's Services and Industries

Dedication

For my daughter, Tracie

My theological reflection began with a question you
once asked. "Daddy, what's God like?" This book is
part of my answer. I know you will understand.

Lord,
Nice Timing!

1 I knew the score when I came through the trap gate of the Tennessee State Prison for men in Nashville that Friday evening, July 18, 1980. Even though this prison had a cruel reputation for human savagery, I was more tired than afraid.

The steel gate makes an unnerving crash when it slams shut. Once those gates close, there's no way back out. You're swallowed up in the belly of an evil beast, cut off and isolated in an environment where men prey on one another like killer sharks in the sea.

I climbed the five flights of stairs to nine walk, nineteenth cell, where I was assigned in D Block. In trying to make the prison environment more civilized, prison officials had renamed all the blocks as "units." But prison traditions don't die that easily. The cell block smelled of disinfectant, dust, and the sour odor of human fear trapped in a cage. I was glad to be in the nineteenth cell—it was the last one on the tier. That gives a person fighting room (if it comes to that) without having to worry about his back.

When a prisoner first steps behind the walls, he *knows* he's going to be tried on for size by somebody within a few days of arrival. There's no maybe about it. The only law in the concrete-and-steel jungle of any prison is survival of the fittest, hammered and hacked out in the most barbaric, cruel, and ruthless terms.

When nothing happened during the first week I began to relax. Two bloody murders occurred—one right in front of me. But I hoped my six-foot-two-inch, 220-pound frame might discourage any reckless adventures from the penitentiary sharks.

But three men stopped in front of my cell door the following Friday afternoon. I didn't recognize any of them. One man pulled a shank* out from under his shirt and held it up for me to look at. So much for wishful thinking!

"Ya see this, chump?" he growled, lightly running his finger over the polished, wicked-looking blade. From years of experience in working the streets as a detective, I suspected he was flying high on some dope, probably speed.

I nodded without speaking.

"Wassa matta, chump? You don't talk too good?"

"I can talk all right."

Another kid pushed his face closer to the door. He looked about 19, with long, stringy brown hair, and his arms were covered with crude prison tattoos. Later I learned his brains were scrambled from huffing too much glue.

"Ya eitha set out ya watch and ring, or we're gonna cut ya heart out and bite it while it's still pumpin'," he giggled.

A blizzard of conflicting ideas and feelings flashed through my mind. I remembered an old convict telling me back at the jail, "There ain't no God behind the walls except a shank and a lead pipe. Stand on your

---

* Prison slang for a homemade 5- to 10-inch knife, usually made in the prison metal shop.

own two feet, and don't *ever* back up from anybody. Not even an inch! If you back up one time, you'll spend the rest of your life in the joint traveling in reverse."

I looked at my wedding band. Although it had long since lost any symbolic value to me, I kept it as a reminder. Staring at the three thieves, I tried to sort out my feelings. How is a Christian supposed to respond to such an encounter? Ethical issues debated back in academy and college weren't designed for such an event.

"I think you lads would be better off going somewhere else," I suggested, trying to keep the bile of anger out of my voice.

The crazy one began to cackle in a high-pitched voice. "Did ju hear 'im? He thinks we oughtta go away."

"I'm personally gonna cut you up bad if you don't hand that ring and watch out," the first man snarled.

I nodded. "Maybe so."

He looked puzzled. "Are you crazy or somethin'! I'm gonna cut your head off and set it in the sink!" he screamed, waving the knife in the air.

"You might," I admitted, stalling for time. "But you know as well as I do it's not that easy to kill a man with a knife when he's not real thrilled with the idea. You *might* kill me. But, then again, you might just lose that blade. Who knows what might happen in a free-for-all donnybrook?"

The crazy one peered at me suspiciously. "What's a donnybrook? You gotta piece?" *

I didn't answer.

The three men looked at one another, confused about what to do next. The robbery wasn't going right.

* Prison slang for pistol.

11

I was a new buddy,* supposedly an easy mark for the robber gangs that roam the prison.

The three thieves left the walk, promising to get me when I came out for chow. When the guard opened my cell door 30 minutes later, I stepped out onto the walk, keeping my hand in my pocket. Although I wasn't holding anything more deadly than a handful of sweat, nobody else knew that. The guard looked at me curiously when I remained standing in front of my cell, waiting for the swirling 400-man mass to exit the cellblock. I'd heard of men being dropped in a crowd by an unknown assailant, the rest unaware he was hit until he fell over with a piece of steel hanging out of his back.

Knowing the prison system well enough to realize that he wouldn't be any help, I ignored the guard. Even if he was willing to interfere, I couldn't yell for help from a guard and expect to walk the prison yard later—at least not and live to tell about it!

As I went through the main entrance of the cellblock, I saw the crazy one about 20 yards ahead of me, standing up against the wall of the chow hall. The second man lurked near the entrance, about 10 yards to my right. I didn't see the third one, but I knew he wouldn't be far away.

Curtly I nodded to the one standing near the door. He looked straight ahead, pretending he didn't see me. The handle of the shank stood out against his shirt. Briefly I flirted with the idea of nailing him right where he stood, getting it all over and done with once and for all. Instead, I took a deep breath and began walking toward the chow hall.

The distance between the main dining room and

* Somebody new to the prison community.

the cellblock was the longest 100 yards I've ever walked. Halfway between the two men I heard the sound of feet scuffling on the concrete behind me. The man hadn't moved—he just wanted to see me run.

But I stopped and waited, looking directly at the kid leaning against the wall. Five seconds passed in silence. Ten seconds. Twenty. I had both hands in my pockets again, and the kid stared at me owlishly, trying to focus on me through his drug-soaked mind.

Men in prison intuitively know when something's "going down," and they stay away from the scene of the action. But I could feel a hundred eyes watching. Silently. Waiting.

The crazy one got fidgety, changing his slouch from one foot to the next, until he began moving away, crablike, keeping his back to the wall until he was well past me. By the time I turned around, I saw the first man duck back inside the cellblock.

Dinner was a lonely affair that evening. Most prison killings take place inside the chow hall, so nobody sat beside me or even *at* the four-man table I so conspicuously occupied in the crowded dining room.

I would have been a lot happier if a legion of those proverbial angels had showed up about then. Instead, I suddenly remembered an obscure passage from Isaiah:

> See, I have refined you,
>   though not as silver;
> I have tested you in the
>   furnace of affliction.*

"Talk about a furnace!" I grumbled silently,

* Isaiah 48:10, NIV.

chewing my food slowly and wiping the sweat off my forehead. "I need a small army, and You give me riddles!"

Nine-walk was deserted when I returned to the cellblock after dinner. Most of the population went to the ball field to escape the stifling heat inside the blocks. Thirty minutes later the same guard came around and opened my cell door and let me go inside. Putting a tape of the Heritage Singers on my stereo, I leaned back against the cool, concrete wall, waiting for the return of the Three Musketeers. I had no doubt they would be back.

"I seem to be caught in a bind, Lord," I silently prayed. "I don't want to hurt anybody, and I'm not real anxious to get killed over something as trivial as a watch and wedding ring. But if I just hand over what they want, I'll have to go through this exercise again and again. I won't be able to walk the yard safely, at least not without constant conflict."

Silence.

As the following hour passed with only the Heritage Singers for company, I felt more than a little forlorn. What was I doing in this human sewer, a million miles away from anything human or sane, serving a 99-year sentence for first-degree murder, caught up in some bizarre time warp straight out of the Twilight Zone!

I looked at my watch. Seven-thirty, EST. Once more I could hear the voices of old friends singing in the Sligo church, even the good-natured grumbling about compulsory chapel attendance. That seemed like a century ago. "If the old gang could see me now," I chuckled sardonically. "They wouldn't believe their eyes!"

"Hey, man! Lemme talk at ya for a minute."

Sitting up on the bunk, I saw the man who had flashed the knife at me earlier. "Here we go again," I sighed.

"Lookie here, we gotta straighten this thing out," he stammered. "Some friends of yours just talked to me, and said they'd have ta do something about me if I didn't lay off you, see?"

"No, I don't see. And I don't know what you're talking about. What friends?"

He looked agitated, fumbling around for words. "Look, this joint ain't big enough so's I gotta be lookin' over my shoulder all the time, wonderin' if you're comin' afta me, or your road dogs* is gunnin' for me, too. So far, ain't nobody got hurt or lost nothin', right? You got heart—I can see that—and you ain't gonna let nobody rob you. I respect that. Let's say you and me call it a draw."

"I still don't know what you're talking about, but that suits me fine. No hard feelings either way."

"I got ya word on it?" he asked suspiciously. "You'll call off your friends?"

"We're square."

He stuck his hand through my cell door, a gesture of trust and goodwill, and locked his wrist and thumbs with mine in a penitentiary-style handshake.

"Those homies† of yours are the biggest and baddest-lookin' dudes I ever seen in my life! I don't want nothin' to do with 'em!" he said, backing away.

"Happy Sabbath," I said.

"Huh? Oh, yeah. You too, Rap." *

* One's pal, a person a crimnal would "run with" on the street, pulling off various crimes together.

† Friends from one's hometown.

I sat down on the bunk, thoroughly puzzled. Then
I remembered another fragment from the Psalms:
The angel of the Lord encamps
around those who fear him,
and he delivers them.[†]
My evening prayer was brief: "Lord, nice timing!"

* A common penitentiary way of speaking to somebody when their name is unknown. Rap comes from the slang term *rap sheet*. Prisoners convicted on the same criminal offense together are referred to as "rap partners."
† Psalm 34:7, NIV.

Ministry in the Belly of the Beast

2 While other small children laughed and played, Nelson Graves had to fight like a cornered, wounded animal, learning to defend himself against the savage, merciless beatings of an alcoholic stepfather.

"He liked to polish off a night of heavy drinking by 'teaching the punk who's boss!'" Graves told me as we talked into the early-morning hours. "He didn't care what he used for a weapon as long as it bloodied me up. As I got older, the beatings got worse. I started running away from home, and then . . ." He shrugged and gestured expansively to the cell walls around him.

It's not surprising the tormented youngster grew up fast, angry, and violent. He understood little of the demented behavior of his parents. Like most abused children, he had assumed their brutality was normal and his own pain richly deserved.

The vicious cycle of a monotonously revolving institutional door began at 10 for him when he went to reform school for being an "unruly and runaway" child. The sadistic violence at home quickly dissolved with the grotesque cruelty of reform school.

"We called it 'gladiator school,'" * he remembered.

* The term *gladiator school* is a common description of juvenile reform schools made by prisoners who "came up through the ranks."

"Trial by ordeal, and survival of the fittest. Even at 10 you gotta learn how to protect yourself from the sharks, or get eaten alive.

"Taft Youth Center was a real animal house a few years ago. Kids got raped, robbed, and beaten regularly by other juveniles. And then they'd get beaten or sexually exploited again by some of the perverted staff members. It was a real trip!" he added with obvious anger and contempt.

By the time he was 18, when I met him for the first time, Nelson Graves fit the classic profile of an adult offender: male, under 25, uneducated, violent, paranoid, an habitual substance abuser (alcohol and drugs), and the product of a poverty-stricken family where child abuse was the norm, not an exception.

Generally, prisoners like Graves have little insight into either their feelings or behavior, and they despairingly describe themselves as "state raised." Early in life, usually before they are 8 or 10 years of age, youngsters like Graves conclude they can't be anybody of stature unless recognized for their criminal achievements. Ironically, they can't make a successful life for themselves, so they end up making the news instead.

The singular difference between youngsters like Graves that come from poverty and abuse, who end up in the criminal justice system, and other youngsters with similar backgrounds who make a success out of their lives, is that successful people almost always have at least one adult role model who took some interest in them. At 18, Graves couldn't think of anybody who had ever loved or cared for him.

At 20, sentenced to 55 years in prison, he wasn't the kind of man most free world people would consider as a good prospect for Christian fellowship! He knew more about the sinister, evil, and deviant human behavior experienced behind prison walls than anybody can know and still remain civilized.

Although he tried to adjust, to get used to the mind-numbing, meaningless drudgery of prison life, his few friends behind the walls could see he was regressing rapidly. Sullen and withdrawn at one moment, he would lash out savagely against guards, and other prisoners the next. Few people recognized the anguished screams of a small boy coming through the rage of the adult. Drugs didn't help, and he was too smart to drink the potentially toxic homemade prison wine. Visitors were infrequent, and mail nonexistent. His family was quite happy to forget about him.

Finally, during the early-morning hours of a chilly fall day in October 1981, he collapsed. His three cell partners awakened to find him sitting on his bunk, staring like a zombie into some dark and forbidding nightmare within, and silently crying. Apprehensively, the men watched him, unsure what direction his private hell would take.

Loneliness, the deadly killer of the human spirit in every prison, was slowly devouring him.

"You'd better go see the chaplain today!" one man told Graves emphatically.

Amos L. Wilson, 51, chief of chaplaincy services for the Tennessee Department of Correction, is a soft-spoken, scholarly veteran prison chaplain and a man of deep religious faith and clear-headed vision. Better than most, he understands the dehumanizing impact of long-term incarceration in a subculture that doesn't make any provision for normal human relationships. Lengthy isolation in such a deviant environment is an open-ended invitation for disaster when the offender eventually leaves prison—as 98 percent of all of them do.

According to Wilson, Graves's lack of visitors or family contact is typical. Only 25 percent of imprisoned men get regular visits from people in the free world. If a man is married when he comes to prison, divorce papers generally follow within one to three years. Visits from friends and family members become increasingly less as time passes. Slowly, the flow of mail drops to a trickle and then stops. Birthdays and holidays become just another meaningless date for most prisoners, a brutal reminder that one has become a nonperson, exiled and abandoned, forgotten in the belly of the beast.

Relationships, not facts, change people. Under the best of circumstances, authentic rehabilitation is impossible when divorced from the experience of redemption, something most people first encounter within the context of warm and caring relationships.

Bringing prisoners and free world Christians together in an environment where normal friendship can nurture significant behavior and value changes has been the principal goal of Wilson's ministry as a prison chaplain. His leadership has encouraged scores of churches to provide religious services and Bible study classes for the convict population across Tennessee. To many prisoners, however, his single greatest achievement is the visitation program he inaugurated in 1972.

"I wanted to establish a visitation program that would provide committed Christians with an opportunity to translate their faith into concrete action which would be meaningful and rewarding for them,"

Wilson told me. "In addition, I knew that prisoners would benefit socially and spiritually by having a mature, regular visitor from the free world."

Nelson Graves didn't realize his life was about to change radically when he finally walked into the chaplain's office looking for help.

Douglas Faulkner, 53, an engineer with the Nashville Electric Service, and his wife, Nadean, had never given any serious thought to prison ministry until Conn Arnold, a Seventh-day Adventist Church official and volunteer prison chaplain, preached at their church one Sabbath and told the congregation about the opportunity for a special kind of ministry at the state prison.

"I didn't have the training to be a preacher or a Bible teacher," Douglas, a warm and cheerful man, chuckles today. "But I knew we could offer friendship. Nadean was skeptical about the idea at first, but she wanted to examine the possibilities directly."

The first meeting between the Faulkners and Nelson Graves was stiff.

"After several days of intense orientation and training, a half dozen of us free world couples met in a small room with an equal number of prisoners," Douglas recalled. "We spent a few minutes talking with each prisoner, and then David Philipy [assistant chaplain in charge of the program in 1981] had us fill out a form, indicating whom we would like to visit.

"I can't tell you why, but I liked Nelson on sight," Douglas says. "I could tell he was deeply troubled, very suspicious, and paranoid. But we decided to treat him as if he were our own son and let him open up whenever—if ever—he wanted to."

"I expected a lot of prying questions," Nelson

admits. "But they never asked me anything about my charge [the offense for which he was convicted] or how much time I was doing. I didn't think they were for real. I kept waiting for the religious sales pitch."

He laughed. "I guess it's a good thing I didn't hold my breath waiting for them to say or do something to anger me. They respected my right to privacy, and they lived their faith so well they didn't have to talk about it."

One discernable change in the young convict's behavior was swift and dramatic. Within weeks of his first visit with the Faulkners he stopped getting disciplinary write-ups, which for years had made the "hole" (an isolation cell) his second home in prison.

Spending every Saturday afternoon on the prison picnic area (reserved as a privilege for prisoners who work and maintain a good behavior pattern), and fixing a home-cooked meal over a grill with his adopted family and their children became his lifeline with the normal world. "Those three or four hours out there with them is the only time during the week I feel really human," Graves frankly confesses. "I'd rather cut off my arm than miss that time."

At first he was cynical about the Faulkners' interest in him. But as he began to realize they loved him just for himself, that they didn't come to see him in order to impose their ideas of change and improvement upon him, the massive, unbreachable wall he had put up to protect himself against the adult world began to dissolve.

For the first time he saw what a loving family was like, and he wanted to be a part of something in which people cared for one another without any of the violence and betrayal so common to his own life. In

22

them, he was beginning to encounter God's grace. Three years after that unpromising meeting in Chaplain Wilson's office, Nelson Graves decided he wanted to become a part of the Faulkners' religious family, too.

During a deeply emotional service, held in the prison chapel on a warm Sabbath afternoon, April 7, 1984, the entire Faulkner family watched Nelson step into the baptismal tank with their pastor, Eugene Johnson. It was the pastor's first baptism behind the prison walls—but it wouldn't be the last. Douglas remembered Chaplain Philipy's words during their first orientation: "Always remember that you are mediators of God's grace to the prisoners you befriend."

Another prisoner, an old friend of Graves who attended the ceremony, looked at me and shook his head. "I see it," he admitted, "but I still don't believe it!"

When Grace
Strikes

3 Tony was six months into his parole from the Nevada State Prison when he decided to leave Las Vegas. He didn't know where he was going, or even why the sudden compulsion to take off. That old, familiar, black mood of despair was suffocating him again.

"Have you got some kind of crazy death wish?" his girlfriend, Sandy, screamed as he left. "They'll catch you and lock you up in prison again."

But she was talking to an empty door. A cold chill swept over her as she realized she would probably never see him alive again.

Eighteen hours after leaving Sandy, Tony drove into Salt Lake City, bleary-eyed and wasted from the mixture of whiskey, beer, and reefer he'd ingested during the trip. It was January 20, 1979. Eleven days later he arrived in Nashville, Tennessee—broke and confused. Now he had exactly 43 cents in his pocket and a pistol stuck in his belt. Somewhere between Salt Lake City and Nashville he'd lost his new pickup truck and $1,200 in cash. He didn't know how or where.

Tony Larson, age 24, knew how to do only a couple of things. Since his eleventh birthday, he had spent less than three years free on the streets, and never for more than six months at a time. Within minutes he found a car with the keys left in the ignition, and was on his way to the first of three armed robberies for the day.

Several blocks from the last robbery a police squad car pulled in behind him and flipped on the blue lights. The chase was on and it didn't end until 40 miles later, when Tony plastered himself and his stolen car against a concrete overpass. As it turned out, the stolen car belonged to a Nashville police officer! The officers were none too gentle in removing him from the twisted wreckage of the vehicle.

In September 1979, Tony arrived at the Tennessee State Prison. The bones of his left leg were fused together from the ankle to the knee and he needed a cane to walk. He had copped out for a 10-year sentence in prison in exchange for dropping his lawsuit against the county hospital that botched the treatment of his left leg. His disability left him angry, bitter, and hostile.

I remember the first time Tony and his cell partner, Johnny Freeman, walked into the remotivation class I was teaching in the prison school on Sabbath afternoon. Although he didn't make much noise, other convicts quickly got out of his way. There was something mean, surly, and evil about him. They hadn't nicknamed him Troglodyte at the Carson City Prison for his warmth or benevolence.

That kid has a real death wish, I thought to myself. He looked more like a demonic refugee from hell than a man in his mid-20's. A bright red bandanna tied across his forehead kept his long brown hair out of an angry and sneering face. A barbarian straight out of Attila the Hun's army, covered in crude prison tattoos and challenging anybody to a fight.

I liked him.

A few weeks later someone stole my tape-recording equipment from the office where I then worked as a recorder in the prison braille class. Although the state paid me a token wage for reading books on tape, the equipment was my own and I couldn't afford to replace it.

Within an hour Tony barged in. "Lookie here, man. It ain't none of my business," he growled, "but you're a solid con, and we'll back your play if you want to go get that recorder back."

"What do you have in mind?" I asked.

He pointed across the street to where Johnny was standing, casually leaning against the wall, and then he patted his side where I could see the outline of a foot-long prison shank.

"You give the word, and we'll go in there, stab up a few of those punks, and get that recorder! Cut off a couple of their heads," he added as an afterthought, "and they won't want to rob you no more."

The logic was impeccable, if not overly civilized!

Happily, by this time, I'd already made my own somewhat less draconian arrangements to get the equipment returned. But I thanked him for his offer because I knew it came out of respect for me. He nodded curtly and walked away without another word.

In the early-morning hours of Thursday, February 5, 1981, Tony and Johnny put the finishing touches on a project they'd been working on for several weeks—escape. After months of carefully observing the garbage truck as it made its rounds on the prison compound, they knew every second of its schedule.

At 9:00 a.m., they secretly made their way to the rear of the chow hall. For several minutes they concealed themselves, anxiously waiting for the guard in the tower to move out of sight. The two prisoners knew everything depended on perfect timing. A few extra seconds either way meant another delay, capture, or even death in the form of a bloody zipper pattern in the chest from the guards' automatic weapons.

Just as they got ready to move, they had to dive for cover under some boxes in order to avoid being seen by Warden Jim Rose and Captain Louie Kirby, who were looking over that area of the compound.

When the officer finally turned away and Warden Rose and Captain Kirby moved out of sight, Johnny raced for the huge dumpster. Twenty minutes later Tony made it across the open 20 yards, undetected and scrambled into the foul-smelling, roach-infested container. He intuitively knew they weren't two ordinary convicts anymore—they were two very dangerous animals determined to escape from a trap, even if they had to kill somebody to do it.

The trap was more than prison walls. It was endless despair lost in time. Johnny, only 23, had a life sentence for first-degree murder, with no possibility of parole for 30 years. While Tony had only 10 years to do, with parole less than three years away, time was also eating away at him. He had squandered half his life behind prison walls.

Within minutes the garbage truck's steel claw slowly lifted the massive dumpster high in the air over its back. As the lid of the dumpster opened, both men fought to maintain their balance so they would land feet first in the truck.

From dozens of earlier surveillances, they knew the truck driver would not use the bone-pulverizing hydraulic compactor until the next stop. In the meantime they feverishly clawed their way to the inside top of the truck. At most they only had two or three minutes in which to dig out a groove for themselves at the top near the back of the truck. They knew they were dead men without that critical space.

Sweat poured off their bodies as the seconds methodically ticked away. They had no thought of turning back. Both men had sworn an oath that once they got inside the truck (dead or alive), they were leaving prison that morning.

The truck began to move. The first compacting came and went without difficulty. They laughed quietly and began to feel the exhilaration a prisoner goes through when he knows the escape is coming off perfectly. Tony reached over and slapped Johnny on the arm. "We're goin', Bro! Tonight we'll have some good whiskey and fine women. We can forget this hellhole forever."

The relief and elation within them kept growing after each compacting episode. Johnny had a couple of broken ribs already, but it was bearable. The worst thing so far was the overpowering stench of the garbage.

"You need a shower, boy!" Johnny growled. They both laughed quietly.

Thirty minutes later they heard the grinding noise of the massive, green metal gates closing behind them as the truck finally exited the prison. After one last stop on the picnic area, it was a nonstop trip to the distant landfill where a waiting friend would pick them up.

29

The hydraulic whine of the compactor lazily began to increase in pitch. As the two men heard the last dumpster smash down on its concrete foundation, the garbage in the truck began slowly shifting backward and up toward the two men lying side by side in their coffin-shaped grooves. But this time the pressure didn't stop—it kept increasing. Tony felt cold sweat breaking out on his chest as he realized they had made a lethal miscalculation. There wasn't going to be any whiskey or fine women for them that night or any night ever again. They were about to be crushed to death.

He heard the snap of his crippled left leg breaking in three or four places just a split second before he felt the mind-numbing pain slashing through his brain. "Tony!" Johnny gasped softly. Bewildered, resigned anguish filled his voice as he whispered again through clenched teeth, "Tony, I'm gone!"

"I'm gone!" That's all there was to it. No screams. No protests. Tony heard the air squeezed out of his friend's lungs and the obscene sound of bones breaking and grinding against the cold metal ceiling. Barely able to breathe, he wondered, almost casually, what it was going to be like to die. Through the years he'd seen dozens of men murdered in different prisons, and now it was his turn to go. The idea had a peculiarly demented logic to it, and he couldn't help laughing. In some strange, irrational way, he felt grimly content that he had not yelled for help. He too would die with his friend.

Suddenly, from deep within the depths of his being, a wordless prayer began forming in his mind. *Lookie here, God. Johnny's gone and on his way up to You. I guess I'm coming, too. At least I hope so.*

Anyway, I hope You don't hold no hard feelings.
Thanks.

Abruptly, the pressure stabilized. The truck lurched forward and began its 30-minute drive to the dump. His body was totally numb from the neck down. He wondered if his back was broken, and it irritated him that death was taking so long. Just as his mind began to drift into darkness, the truck rumbled to a stop and jolted him back to reality. The back end slowly opened, and the garbage containing the broken and twisted refuse from the state prison began spilling out.

Struggling for breath and desperately trying to claw his way to the top of the garbage pile at the same time, Tony finally broke through and saw daylight. Frantically, he looked in every direction for the friend who was supposed to pick him up. Nothing! Nothing but garbage everywhere, and the strangely peaceful-looking, broken rag-doll body of his friend. He knew he'd been betrayed.

Even though his leg throbbed with pain, one of those rare, brilliant flashes of insight seized his consciousness, and he saw clearly what his life added up to. He was nothing but a mashed, stinking bit of life's garbage. For the first time in his life he knew what it was to be afraid, to be seized with a nameless, terrorizing dread. At 26, with 12 years of his life wasted behind prison walls, he wasn't afraid of dying. The real horror and despair came from knowing he wasn't going to escape the misery of his empty existence by death that day. In spite of his best effort he was going to go on living.

He wanted to cry.

When Grace Strikes, Part II
By Tony Larson

I stayed high and drunk for the first week out of the hole. Everybody and his brother patted me on the back for my escape attempt seven months before and laid free dope on me. Even though I didn't draw a sober breath that week, the stuff didn't satisfy me like it used to. It didn't matter if I was stoned or not, I still couldn't forget that cold winter day I spent sprawled over the garbage pile.

I couldn't get rid of the image. Over and over in my mind I heard, *You're nothing but a sack of stinking, human garbage! Useless. A bum!* I felt guilty for Johnny's death. While I knew I wasn't responsible for it, he was dead and I was alive. We were only inches apart!

Most of my time in the hole I spent trying to think of some way to make Johnny's death mean something. I remembered a guy who ripped him off for a gold chain. Under any other circumstances, Johnny would have killed him for that. But we were only days away from our escape and he didn't want to do anything to jeopardize our plans. "Let it go," he'd said to me. "A gold chain ain't worth losing this chance to get away."

But I couldn't let it go, especially not now. In my mind I killed the thief a hundred times. Within an hour of being released from the hole, I got a shank and went looking for him, planning to kill him on sight. No dice—he'd been transferred to another prison, and I was left with my impotent rage.

Then I began doing stupid and reckless things I'd never done in any other joint. I burned everybody—for money, dope, anything I could get my hands on.

When my brain would get to spinning and that black mood of despair struck, I ripped off the dope man for whatever I wanted. And hoped he didn't like it! You don't rip off the dope man in any penitentiary, at least not if you plan to be alive to celebrate your next birthday. I seemed driven to attempt suicide, but at some other man's hand. By this time, however, I had terrorized the prison so thoroughly that nobody would come near me.

Still I kept going to the Saturday afternoon remotivation class. Half the time I was too stoned to learn much, but it was a good place to check out the free world women and get a free pint of ice cream. Conversation swirled around my head in patternless waves. Little registered.

After the opening preliminaries, the class split up into two groups. On one side were the dudes who wanted to talk about getting their heads together in religious terms. Bible texts flew around the room like random golf balls at a driving range. But many of the cons like me didn't know what they were talking about most of the time.

Our group consisted of the Black and White hard cases. We had the roughest bunch of cons in the joint, and Jack coordinated the class. He's a burly Irishman with a desert-dry sense of humor. Unlike the other group teachers, however, Jack wrote his own lessons. It was a trip each week just to check out his zany titles. His lessons and verbal rap were laced with popular song lyrics, poetry, lines from philosophers, and even Bible verses. At first, some of the wise guys tried to play a lot of verbal games with him, but he had a polite way of leading them into intellectual traps they couldn't get out of.

I knew him for six months before I realized he was a Christian. Don't misunderstand me—he wasn't doing anything bad. But he didn't use a lot of God-words or God-talk. And when he did speak about God and religious faith, he spoke easily and comfortably like it was a natural thing, nothing spooky. His deep, personal convictions didn't stand out like a sore thumb.

"If your religious faith is about anything of value," he told me later, "you don't have to be constantly bashing folks over the head with it. The way you live your life, the way you treat other people, the way you make people feel about themselves will be the most profound sermon you ever preach. If you're really walking with God, you don't have to send out a news release to announce the fact. It shows."

"We're condemned to be free, whether we like it or not," he would tell the class. "When we get done with all the bitterness, resentment, and self-pity, that's the bottom line of life. We might not have any control over some of our circumstances, but we always control how we respond to those circumstances. So why not make a life for ourselves, instead of the news? Our lives don't have to be a constant rehearsal of 'meanwhile, back in the lions' den!' Each person, even a prisoner, is one of God's beautiful ideas in the process of growth, and God doesn't make junk."

The men would laugh, but those throwaway lines had a way of sticking in a man's mind all week long. It isn't that he told us anything we didn't know already—he just made it sound like it made sense. "You can't *live* crooked and think straight, and you can't *think* crooked and live straight," he said once, looking me right in the eye.

A couple of months after I got out of the hole, I stooped to a new low by ripping off a good friend for nearly $300. When he confronted me, I just looked at him and said, "Come and take it!" I talked a good line, but deep inside I was hoping he'd knock my brains out. But he didn't, and I felt even more funky.

One day I went up to the 7th Step* office to drink some coffee and shoot the breeze. Jack was working at one of the desks. "Look out! Tony the Tiger is here," he said as I walked in. I didn't know if he was being friendly or just laughing at me.

To this day I can't give a rational explanation for what made me want to talk to him that day. He had always treated me with respect, and I knew other people spoke to him about their problems. In a way, he seemed like a priest, at least what I figured a good priest ought to be like. He just carried himself that way, and I knew for sure I had to talk to somebody and get all the poison out of my system before it killed me.

I wandered all around Robin Hood's barn before I finally blurted, "Hey, Jack, I'd like to talk with you someday when you've got a few minutes."

He stopped typing and looked at me for a few minutes without saying a word. It was a critical, thoughtful examination, almost as though he was considering whether or not I was worth the time. I could have given him the answer to that without all the evaluation!

Suddenly, he got up and headed for the door. "Let's go up on the ball field where we can walk and

---

* An organization, founded in 1963, to help ex-convicts back into society by following seven steps and by providing a support group similar to Alcoholics Anonymous. For further information, see *My Shadow Ran Fast*, by Bill Sands, founder of the 7th Step Foundation.

talk at the same time," he said.

Somebody once said that a journey of a thousand miles begins with the first step. As we started walking around the ball field on that cold November day, I had no idea where it was going to lead me. But for the next few weeks we took many walks, around and around the half-mile track, while I talked and he listened without interruption, except to draw me out or to clarify a point.

I really don't remember exactly what I said, but I know I gave him a pretty grim picture of my life story and all the emptiness and despair that went with it. Nothing seemed to shock him, and I told him things that would make a marble statue shiver!

One day he abruptly stopped and gestured toward the ground ahead of us. "What do you see?" he asked.

His question startled me. "A path," I answered.

"Where does this path take you?"

"Around the ball field."

"No. Listen to my question: *Where* does this path take you?"

"It doesn't take me anywhere," I snapped irritably. "It just goes around and around in circles."

Nodding silently, he smiled as though pleased with my answer, and sat down, cross-legged, and gestured me down, too. He sat on one side of the path, and I sat on the other side facing him. Other men using the circle either had to pass between us or around us, but he didn't seem to notice.

"We have been walking the path of your life, Tony," he said. "That's what we've been doing for the past few weeks. It begins and ends nowhere," he added bluntly. "That's the way it is with every path in life except one. All the other paths go endlessly in circles. You might get drunk, high, or dizzy from all the motion, but that's all you get. Eliot called it:

> Shape without form, shade
>   without colour,
> Paralyzed force, gesture
>   without motion.

"That describes my life in a nutshell, all right," I muttered with disgust. "But I don't know how to change all this craziness, or how to even begin solving my problems."

"No, Tony, that's not the issue," he said. "You don't have a problem to solve—at least not at first. You have a decision, a commitment to make. Now you said you wanted to be free, to be at peace, to straighten out the relationship between you and the mother of your two daughters. But if you truly want all of that, you have to quit taking the easy path of beating yourself over the head for the things you've done in the past. Repentance means a change of direction in your life. Calling yourself names is a cheap copout.

"If you truly want to be free, you must choose to follow the one path that has heart, and then you must walk that path in dignity, without fear *or* ambition."

I felt a strange prickling sensation, and the hair stood up on my arms as he looked directly at me and began reciting lines from Robert Frost:

> I shall be telling this with a sigh
> Somewhere ages and ages hence:
> Two roads diverged in a wood, and I—
> I took the one less traveled by,
> And that has made all the difference.

The sun was slowly disappearing over the western wall

of the penitentiary. I felt energized and frustrated at the same time. The loudspeaker began blasting, "Clear the ball field! Clear the ball field!"

"I don't know what's happening to me," I muttered.

Again he just looked at me thoughtfully, considering, weighing something known only to himself. Then he took out his wallet and carefully removed a folded piece of paper that looked dog-eared and ready to fall apart. I could see something was typed on the page, but he continued staring at it without saying anything.

Then he glanced at me again. "Several years ago I came across some lines from the late theologian, Paul Tillich. These words meant a lot to me at the time, and they have sustained me during critical times in my life. Listen:

"'Grace strikes us when we are in great pain and restlessness.' Tony," he said quietly. "It strikes us when we walk through the dark valley of a meaningless and empty life. . . . It strikes us when, year after year, the longed-for perfection of life does not appear, when the old compulsions reign within us as they have for decades, when despair destroys all joy and courage. Sometimes at that moment a wave of light breaks into our darkness and it is as though a voice were saying: 'You are accepted, accepted by that which is greater than you, and the name of which you do not know. Do not ask for the name now; perhaps you will find it later. Do not try to do anything now; perhaps later you will do much. Do not seek for anything; do not intend anything. Simply accept the fact you are accepted.'"

During a special service of the Adventist Freedom Fellowship, exactly two years from the date of my fatal escape attempt, almost to the very hour—on Saturday, February 5, 1983—Elder Conn Arnold and I stepped into the frigid water of the baptismal tank in the prison chapel. There he recited the ancient rite, "I now baptize you in the name of the Father, and of the Son, and of the Holy Spirit. Amen."

How did I get from the garbage pile to the baptismal tank? God sent a man into prison who showed me a world that I didn't even know existed. For 18 months Jack and I walked and talked. When I felt discouraged and wanted to give up, he would remind me that grace strikes us when the longed-for perfection of life does not appear, when the old compulsions reign within us, when despair destroys all joy and courage.

I thought Jack was just a strange, enigmatic character who dropped into this prison out of nowhere. But then he introduced me to some of his free world friends: Elder Conn Arnold and his wife, Dot, for instance. He began visiting me when I got sent back to the hole for leading a work strike. That man loved me and trusted me, even when I kept letting him down. It was hard enough trying to figure out what made Jack tick, and now there were two of them.

Then Jerry and Louise Willis started writing to me. Other people sent me stamps. A little boy from Kentucky sent me his Bible. Conn gave me a tape recorder so Jack and I could keep up with our rap sessions. I didn't know people like this even existed. Certainly, I never knew any other convict in my life who had friends like this.

My life had been going to hell in a pushcart fast, and prison and solitary confinement, or even eloquently articulated theology didn't change the direction. It changed in response to the people who came to love me and who wanted me to love them back.

On June 15, 1983, I walked through the front gates of the prison a free man. Later that evening I sat in the Madison Campus church in the midst of 150 strangers who made themselves my friends and watched Sandy and my oldest daughter get baptized. An hour later, Elder Conn Arnold married Sandy and me.

This isn't the end—it's a new beginning on a long and difficult road.

The Banker
Goes to Prison

4 Tennessee's banking industry shook to the foundations in 1983 when the Knoxville-based banking empire of Jake Butcher suddenly collapsed like a house of cards, setting in motion a chain reaction of failure in a score of smaller banks connected with him. It was one of the largest bank failures since the Great Depression; more than 7,000 people sustained uninsured losses in excess of $50 million.

Like angry bees, federal bank examiners and FBI agents swarmed over the bank's records, beginning the tedious process of unraveling evidence of massive theft and bank fraud committed by Butcher and his cronies. In November 1984 the disgraced financier, once one of the most respected and powerful political figures in the state, twice running for governor and touted as "Tennessee's national treasure" in 1978 by President Jimmy Carter, entered federal court, in handcuffs, to face a long list of criminal charges.

In October, a month before a federal grand jury indicted Butcher, another Tennessee banker, Edwin Gus "Eddie" Armstrong, 35, a collateral specialist for 13 years with the Nashville City Bank, entered the maximum security state prison for men in Nashville for the first time.

No screaming headlines announced the event.

"I always figured bankers belonged in prison," one inmate chuckled gleefully after meeting Armstrong in the prison chapel. "He looks pretty good in stripes, too!"

But Eddie, as he prefers to be called, didn't go behind the massive stone walls of Tennessee's most dangerous prison to serve time on a prison sentence. Instead he came to begin a monthly preaching assignment for the Adventist Freedom Fellowship. His "stripes" consisted of a conservatively cut, pin-stripe suit.

The young banker doesn't look like the proverbial busy man. Instead, he's a relaxed, warm, and gracious man who resembles an athlete, which he is, more than a banker. (In 1979, sponsored by his bank, he ran the 26.2-mile Boston Marathon in 2 hours and 57 minutes.) People remember him for his quick smile and the attentive, interested way in which he listens to those talking with him. And he never appears to be in a hurry, no matter how crowded his calendar gets.

"Eddie isn't flashy, he's just steady," says a friend who described the busy schedule of outreach activities Armstrong engages in for the First Seventh-day Adventist Church in Nashville. "He gets so much done because he loves serving the Lord. He likes helping people, and he's learned to pace himself.

"I praise the Lord for all he's blessed me with," Armstrong said simply as we talked recently in a conference room adjacent to the prison chapel. "I have a wonderful wife and two beautiful daughters (Andra, 8 and Sara, 4), many friends, and a great career. What more could a man hope for?"

But he is quick to admit his life hasn't always been

either so full or happy.

After fifteen years of bitter conflict, a tumultuous era of social and political upheaval staggered to a confused, weary, and anticlimactic end in 1975. Eddie and Julie Armstrong, then approaching their mid-20s and five years of marriage together, were like most young couples who grew up during the turbulent sixties and early seventies.

"Julie and I were both raised as Baptists," he told me. "While I suppose we were cultural Christians, religion really didn't mean much to me. I'd come to hate God because of what I'd been taught as a boy about eternal hell. I didn't think a God who would punish and torment sinners forever in a lake of fire was either a good God or One who should be taken seriously."

In May he took off from work and struck out on a cross-country bicycle trip. He hoped the grueling exercise and time away from his job would help him sort out his growing disillusionment with life. During the trip he picked up a copy of *Foods for Fitness* to read during rest stops. It described Seventh-day Adventists as people who followed a vegetarian diet.

Adventists! he thought. *Aren't they sort of weird?* Dismissing the thought, he got on with the race.

While Eddie buried his restless anxiety in work and marathon running, Julie's footsteps turned in a direction that would bring the young couple into a deeper crisis and radically alter both their lives.

"My sister, Loretta Tamba, went to a Kenneth Cox evangelistic crusade in 1974," Julie recalled. "When he came back the following year, she invited me to go with her. Even though I was a Christian, the crusade was a deeply moving spiritual experience for me. I had so many questions, but for the first time I saw the character of God more clearly. Religious issues such as righteousness by faith, the Sabbath, the second coming of Christ, life after death, and prophetic events suddenly came into sharper focus as I listened to Elder Cox preach. It was like a big puzzle that was suddenly solved."

Julie was baptized in August, but Eddie refused to attend the service. "I didn't care about her going to the meetings or even joining the church," he said. "But we had an ugly fight—I was the one who got ugly—when she said she was going to tithe her income."

He shook his head ruefully as he remembered their conflict. "Giving away 10 percent of your income is going to get the unqualified attention of *any* banker!"

In spite of his apparent indifference to religion, Julie knew her husband to be a thoughtful and sensitive man, so she didn't badger him about her new religious community. "But a lot of people were praying for him," she admits with a smile.

"I was curious about Adventists," Eddie says today. "That's why I finally went to church with her one Sabbath. I wanted to find out why she joined that church. Secondly, I remembered what I'd read about Adventists in *Foods for Fitness*. As an amateur athlete, I wanted to know more about this health issue. Finally, as I got to know Elder Nathan Sims and other Adventists Julie associated with, I had to admit they were an exceptionally warm and attractive group of people."

A methodical and thorough man, Armstrong plunged into a detailed study of his wife's religious convictions. He didn't think it would take much effort to demolish her beliefs. While she washed clothes one evening at the laundromat, he sat in his van with a pen, pad, and Bible, taking careful notes as he listened to a series of Cox's tapes.

"Once I got past trying to disprove her religious beliefs with the Bible, I discovered I had two burning questions of my own," he said. "I had to know if Jesus actually existed as a person. Elder Cox provided overwhelming evidence that He was, in fact, a historical figure. Then I had to know if Jesus was who He claimed to be. When it became clear to me that He was, I found myself facing a more challenging, personal question: How would I respond?"

Most men like to think of their response to life's ultimate questions as exclusively intellectual. But on a deeply human level the hard-headed banker felt himself equally attracted to the thoughtful, friendly, and Christ-centered Sabbath school class taught by Pastor Sims for visitors.

"I enjoyed that class more than any religious service I've ever attended," he said quietly. "I never learned much in any other church, but Elder Sims wasn't afraid of tough questions. He liked to explore important issues in depth, and his convictions were rooted solidly in the Bible."

In that Sabbath school class, Julie, Elder Sims, and other members of the church became important mediators of God's grace for Eddie Armstrong. "When Nathan finally made a call one Sabbath, I found myself praying, 'Lord, I've tried everything else. I want to be a part of Your family, but I don't want to be a pew warmer. *Give me something to do!*'"

Eddie was baptized in October, only two months after Julie. "It was the most important miracle I've ever seen," Julie said, her eyes glistening.

Eddie Armstrong was never in any danger of becoming a simple pew warmer. God quickly answered his prayer for something to do.

"He plunged in with both feet, a new Christian who was on fire for the Lord," recalls Douglas Faulkner, then the first elder of the church. "It didn't take long before people realized he's a gifted Bible teacher."

"I never thought of myself as a teacher or a public speaker," Armstrong frankly admits. "I used to be painfully shy and nervous in group situations, but Elder Sims was determined to put me to work anyway."

"Eddie is the kind of church member every minister dreams about," says his pastor, Elder Eugene Johnson. "He's served the church as an elder, the director of personal ministries, and a popular Sabbath school teacher. Recently he and Charley Hayes, also a new church member, began producing a daily radio show, *Answers From Scriptures*, for WNAH-AM. The men at the prison seem to enjoy his 'teaching style' of preaching, and I don't even know how many different Bible studies he has going at the moment."

"It's been amazing to me how Eddie has evolved," Julie laughed. "I had no idea he had such skills."

"Julie is the kind of wife every man should be blessed with," Eddie said, looking at his wife of 15 years with obvious warmth and affection. "She's the stability in my life."

Two events during the recent past have added rich meaning to Armstrong's life. First, friends and colleagues at the bank asked him to conduct a weekly Bible study for them. The group, consisting of professional people from various denominations, meets each Wednesday during the lunch hour in the bank's boardroom.

"I've known Eddie for 10 years and he's highly thought of around this bank," said Robert Fouch, the vice president for Nashville City Bank. "His religious beliefs are well known, and he's respected for them."

Even when Eddie received a promotion to top management in the bank, he said the Wednesday Bible study in the boardroom would continue.

The second event was both sobering and exhilarating. His brother called him one night and asked if he could spare one evening each week for a series of Bible studies with him and other family members.

"He was surprised that family members wanted him to give them Bible studies," says a friend. "But those who know Eddie weren't surprised at all. He has that kind of integrity."

Death Sentence

Part I

5 Rhonda Green, 18, a high school senior, employed as a part-time convenience store clerk in Kingsport, Tennessee, had a happy Christmas celebration with her family in 1980. Life was full to the brim and overflowing for her. A popular young woman in school, intelligent and attractive, she dreamed about all the things most girls her age think about: going to college in the fall, getting married, and raising a family of her own.

As she opened her presents on Christmas Eve, she didn't know that two thieves were sitting in a bar 500 miles away, getting drunk, and at that very moment plotting a series of robberies that would end in her murder.

On the afternoon of January 18, 1981, Rhonda left home for the last time and walked the few blocks between home and the Mr. Jiffy where she worked. A meticulous person, she kept her room looking like something out of *Good Housekeeping:* neat, very feminine. She would never see it again.

At the same time, several miles away, Ronald R. Harries, 29, on his twenty-eighth day of freedom, after serving a 10 year sentence for armed robbery and kidnapping in the Ohio State Penitentiary, sat on the passenger side of the car, telling stories about his life of crime while his friend drove cautiously around Kingsport, looking over the targets they'd selected as good robbery prospects.

Harries opened the car window and flung an empty whiskey bottle to the pavement, grinning quietly when he heard the smashing of shattered glass. He liked smashing things. An explosive anger clung to him like a heavy cloak.

The two men were dangerously intoxicated from a deadly mixture of liquor and speed. Harries was an addict and needed several hits each day. They stopped briefly at a vacant lot, and the youthful looking ex-con gently inserted the needle into a vein in his left arm, smiling softly, looking boyish and contented when the rush hit him.

"Ah, that's good stuff," he muttered, smacking his lips. "Now let's go knock off that Mr. Jiffy joint. I need a good lick."*

Customers came and went that evening, buying small odds and ends, so Rhonda had plenty of time to talk with Linda, a cousin who also worked in the store. Nothing serious. Just girl talk about family, boyfriends, and life in the small East Tennessee town they called home.

It surprised her when Harries walked through the front door. The parking lot was empty, so most customers parked directly in front of the store. If Harries had a car, she couldn't see one. Perhaps she felt some mild alarm. The electric clock on the wall hummed quietly as he walked slowly through the store, the minute hand lazily, indifferently, methodi-

---

* To score, to get some money.

cally ticking off the last few seconds of the young woman's life.

He looked Rhonda over carefully, expertly measuring her for any sign of danger. His eyes swept the small store. Since the age of 9, he had spent nearly 20 years of his life confined in dark prison cages where a man lived by his wits—or died. Uncomfortable and curiously threatened in the presence of the silent teenager, he felt like an animal out of familiar territory.

Finally he nodded and smiled through thin lips. She didn't pose any threat, and he didn't see anybody else in the store. But an irrational sense of anger and hostility toward the waiting girl stirred within him. The drug-induced euphoria suddenly clouded.

Suddenly he shuddered from some deeply-rooted but unknown terror. Blinking as though shaking off the grotesque picture forming in his mind, he stepped up to the cash register, jerked the pistol from under his coat, and pointed it directly between Rhonda's terrified eyes.

She gasped and froze. The nightmare of every convenience store clerk was beginning. Time began to telescope as she looked into his cold, blue eyes. Her smile vanished, leaving behind a twisted mask. Seconds took hours to pass, and the barrel of the pistol looked like a huge, black, unblinking eye.

"Gimme all your money," Harries commanded harshly. "And put it in that small bag," he barked, pointing to a stack of grocery bags. His speech was surprisingly clear, considering all the alcohol and drugs he'd ingested during the past few days. But he felt like an actor outside of himself, reading lines from a script. The girl was terrified, probably wondering if he would just leave, rape her, or kill her. He loved the power he held over her while loathing himself at the same time.

It don't take much to scare a kid when you got a pistol, he thought to himself in disgust.

Rhonda didn't hesitate to do as she was told. All she wanted to do was give him the money and have him gone. His pale-blue eyes frightened her. Something evil and sinister radiated from him in waves, and she shivered when she saw the crudely drawn prison tatoo of a naked dagger on his right forearm. Another tatoo decorated his right bicep, but she didn't see that. It might have puzzled her. Contained within the outline of a scroll was the name Rhonda, and a date, November 4, 1970.

Suddenly Harries tensed. Later he would say he thought he heard somebody shout in back of the store and that startled him. The pistol, still pointed directly at Rhonda's head, exploded. The impact of the bullet in her brain spun her around before she crumpled to the floor. Blood matted her shiny, copper hair.

Linda heard the sound from the stockroom where she was marking prices on produce. She rushed to the door without thinking, and stopped short within a few feet of where Harries stood staring stupidly at the body of the dying girl.

The killer whirled and fired again in the direction of the sound, and a slug smashed into the door frame beside her. She froze and, stunned, stared at the growing pool of blood under her cousin's head. *This is a dream, a nightmare,* she thought to herself. *I'll wake up in a minute.* But she didn't. Seconds ticked off as Harries and Linda looked at each other.

"I didn't come in here to hurt anybody," Harries

snarled, leaping up on top of the counter. His voice was low and ominous. "Gimme the money in the cash register and the safe," he commanded.

Linda stumbled forward woodenly, nearly falling when she tripped over Rhonda's body. The critically wounded girl was breathing hoarsely, and blood continued gushing from the wound in her head.

Only minutes passed from the time the killer fled the scene and Rhonda's father rushed into the store, where he found his only daughter lying on the floor in a slowly spreading pool of blood. She died later that evening without ever regaining consciousness.

The robbery netted the two thieves approximately $1,500, which they divided equally between themselves. The police captured the fleeing killer six days later without a fight in Tampa, Florida. His accomplice had turned him in to detectives in exchange for immunity from prosecution.

"I never meant to kill her. It was an accident. You can believe that!" he protested at his trial.

But the jury didn't believe him. Harries personified the malignant cancer of criminality, and people wanted him surgically excised. Before the year was out, the small community tried him, found him guilty, and condemned him to death in the electric chair, dubbed "Ole Sparky" by convicts at the main prison in Nashville.

The death sentence came as no surprise to anybody, including Harries. His life consisted of an uninterrupted and dreary history of criminal acts and prison sentences. From childhood the trajectory of his life was on a collision course with murder and execution.

Today Harries is one of more than 50 men

incarcerated on death row in Tennessee. With one exception, all the men have been desperately fighting for their lives through a tangled, intricate legal process that can take from 6 to 10 years in state and federal courts. Most of them will ultimately be put to death despite their desperate clinging to hope.

Ronald R. Harries was the one exception, stunning his lawyers when he announced in February 1983 that he was ending all further appeals. He ordered his attorneys to refrain from further litigation on his behalf. I thought he was grandstanding. His life had been a mockery, and he wanted to die the same way, thumbing his nose at the whole world.

On Monday, March 12, 1984, I entered Unit VI, the maximum security bunker containing death row prisoners, to interview Harries for the second time. While I waited for the guards to bring him to a small office only a few feet away from the execution chamber, I wondered if he'd changed any since talking to me a year earlier. Although I am opposed to the death penalty, I also have a daughter of my own. I know how I would feel if he'd shot mine to death.

He smiled shyly, almost timidly, when he shook hands with me. His hand was cool and dry and his complexion had an unhealthy, sickly-looking palor from being confined too long without fresh air and sunshine. Because he'd lost so much weight, his clothes hung on him. With painful and vivid clarity, I remembered how I looked after nearly three years of solitary-style confinement.

Behind his cordial mask I saw flashes of a hunted animal trapped inside the man who would be executed in exactly 89 days. "There but for the grace of God go I," flashed into my mind. I knew my own jury would have sentenced me to death, instead of 99 years, if they'd had the option. Brushing the disturbing memory from my mind, I showed him the letter from the editor of *Insight*, expressing interest in a story of his life.

He looked out the window for a few seconds. "Adventists, huh?" he mused. "They're good people. If I can help one young person take a second look at life around him, I guess it will be worth it," he said quietly.

"Fire away. I'll tell you anything you want to know."

The Making of a Killer, Part II

"I can remember being a little kid of 6 or 7," he said, "and my uncles would praise me, saying, 'You're gonna be just like your old man: slick, quick, a good talker.' It seems ironic in retrospect. Both my father and stepfather were murdered.

"My father spent 24 years in different prisons around the country. All my uncles, too, were what you'd call career criminals.

Before going on, he paused a moment, a rueful, sad smile playing around the corners of his mouth. "When I was a little boy, I wanted to be just like my father. He was my hero. Even though he was in and out of prison while I was growing up, I still was proud of him. He was tough and strong, and I wanted his approval."

Harries was born during the cold winter months of 1950 on the south side of Cleveland, Ohio, a decrepit and run-down slum section of the city, populated by a mixture of poor Whites, Blacks, and other ethnic minorities. Smoke from the steel mills behind the projects kept everything looking gray and dingy.

Fronting the projects were an endless string of vegetable markets, warehouses, and bars and taverns where the poor could buy cheap booze, drugs, or sex—anything to escape the grim, grinding reality of their poverty-stricken lives.

His young mother was desperately poor, barely surviving on ADC money from the state, while her con-artist husband wandered in and out of prison. When he finished a prison term, he came home, stayed drunk, and beat his wife unmercifully while his son watched in silence until he couldn't take it anymore. The boy ran away from home for days at a time, wandering the streets and sleeping wherever he could. Violence became a natural part of his life.

"I remember my dad coming home from prison one time with a bottle of whiskey under one arm and a record album under the other. He put the album on and played the same song over and over again: "Your Cheating Heart." While listening to the music, he alternated between drinking from the bottle and beating on my mother. He would have beat her to death if he hadn't passed out first."

Harries spent his early years learning how to hustle, fight, and survive on the streets and in the back alleys. Like children everywhere, whether raised in a palace or the ghetto, he wanted to be accepted, to be a part of something meaningful. So he naturally drifted into one of the local turf-gangs in the community—the Dago Bombers.

"Lincoln Park was the community center," he told me. "That's a fancy name for a sleazy and grubby collection of trees and bushes where our gang hung out. I was too little to join the real fighting between the gangs at first, but I got to carry the baseball bats, chains, chokers, and zip guns the bigger kids used in a rumble.

"My father taught me how to panhandle real good. Since I was quick and good at coming up with the money, the gang leaders would let me hustle on the streets for them, conning people out of nickles and dimes so we could get the winos to buy some Mad Dog or Thunderbird wine for us to drink.

"I guess I was an alcoholic by the time I was 9 or 10 years old. I didn't know it at the time—I just liked to stay blasted, and so did everybody else I knew. We didn't do anything in moderation. By the time I was 12 or 13, I knew more about street drugs than a pharmacist."

His first brush with the law came at 9 years of age. Because of constant truency from school, the courts declared him to be incorrigible, a youngster too wild for his mother to manage. He spent the next two years bouncing in and out of one juvenile detention center after another. Here, as with Nelson Graves, his education in human depravity began in earnest.

Juvenile reform schools are even more wretched than most adult prisons. Every prisoner I've met has admitted that—at its very worst—adult prisons are much safer and saner than reform school. A kid who didn't know how to fight and defend himself got a crippling education in what it's like to be a small fish among the sharks.

"I don't even remember how many gang rapes or beatings I've seen in those places," Harries admitted. "But I was luckier than most kids. Being locked up was no big deal in my family. *Everybody* went to prison, sooner or later, so my father and his brothers taught me how to survive and take care of myself when it was

57

my time to go.

"When I got locked up at some place, I'd find the biggest and toughest-looking kid there," Harries said. "Then I'd walk up and jump all over him. I probably took more beatings than I gave, but it didn't matter whether or not I won the fight. People learned real quick I wouldn't take nothin' off nobody!"

His first criminal conviction came at 11 years of age. He stole a piggy bank containing less than two dollars. Off he went to reform school for two years.

"We called it gladiator school," he told me. "This is where the men got separated from the boys. Survival of the fittest was the only law. Every kid had to prove his manhood—or lose it forever. A kid could only keep what he was strong and mean enough to hang on to.

"Do you have any idea what it's like for a little kid to lay awake in his bunk all night long, every night for two years or more, terrified that some of the bigger kids will rape him before the night is over? *Do you know what that feels like?*"

I had to admit I couldn't even imagine those kinds of feelings. He paused and lit a cigarette. His hand shook, his memory clearly blistered 20 years later by those grotesque memories of his childhood.

"I saw my first murder at 16. My friend was standing in front of me in the chow hall, and another kid walked up and shoved a sharpened spoon into his chest. He bled to death right in front of me. I was scared to death! I thought they were going to kill me, too, because I was his friend. I haven't had many friends since then."

But that was only the first of many killings Harries would see during his life. Between 9 and 30 years of age, he spent less than 37 months outside of a correctional institution. The revolving door of reform school quickly gave way to a larger, faster revolving door in adult prisons. Violence and death became routine.

"After a while, nothing shocks you anymore. Think about it. How many times can you get upset or shocked when people are getting stabbed and beaten to death every other day? Somebody could walk up and kill that man outside the door," he said, pointing to another prisoner we could see, "and I wouldn't even skip a word while talking to you. You can get used to anything when you don't have any other choice."

He was married on January 5, 1970, while home on leave from the Marine Corps. Eleven months later, on November 4, 1970, his daughter was born. The proud parents named her Rhonda. By then he had been dishonorably discharged from the Marines for his arrest and conviction for an armed robbery committed while on leave.

Harries is typical of thousands of young men I've met in prison. His early role models were criminal relatives. They taught him everything he knew about the morals and values of the criminal subculture. Early in life he accepted his role as a criminal and in that role he sought recognition. The only real difference between Graves and Harries is that Graves met some people who cared about him before it was too late.

"I'm institutionalized now," Harries candidly admits. "Eighteen months is the longest stretch I've been on the streets since I was 9. That's when I got married and my two children were born. If they let me out of here tomorrow, I know it would be only a question of time before I'd commit another crime. All the years of drug addiction, heavy drinking, and ripping people off has turned me into a human predator."

Suddenly, becoming tense and agitated, he grabbed my arm. "Jeris, I don't know what's wrong with me anymore. I can sit here and carry on a rational conversation with you right now. But five minutes from now, when I'm back there on the row, I switch gears, play the fool, lie, steal, cheat, con anybody out of anything for no other reason than to be doing it."

Visibly uncomfortable at such an outburst, he sat back and nervously puffed on his cigarette. Being "out of control" frightened him more than being executed.

"How did I become a killer?" he asked, finally repeating my question. A wistful look crossed his face, a flickering recognition that he'd missed something of priceless value during his life, a disturbing realization that his adult role models, particularly the father he loved and admired, had betrayed him and he wasn't smart enough to have figured it out in time.

"I grew up with a lot of hate and fear, the only two emotions I've known and trusted for most of my life," he said quietly. "It takes a lot of liquor and dope to drown those two demons. After a while there ain't enough dope in the world to kill off the pain they cause.

"I'll give you Doc Harries' prescription on how to destroy a kid's life with absolute finality, " he said fiercely. "Raise 'em in an environment that is almost certain to rot every moral sense. Then let the kid run wild, with too little or too much discipline. Be a living role model for hypocritical, deviant, or criminal behavior. And finally, let the kid use drugs and booze as he pleases.

"That's my life in a nutshell," he said after a pause.

"I'm just glad I found something else to heal the pain before I'm executed."

From Out of the Ashes on Death Row, Part III

The camera's cold and unblinking eye impersonally panned over the prison cell block. Over the din of mangled and distorted human voices, echoing off concrete and steel walls, intermingling with the metallic jangle of medieval-sized jailer keys and the hollow reverberating crash of steel on steel, the voice of an unidentified black prisoner said, "I keep asking myself, What am I doing here?"*

For Ron Harries, as the days before his execution grew shorter and he awaited transfer to the death watch cell, the question came during the quiet hours, when the bunker-style cell block for condemned men had retired to a sullen and restless sleep, and he found himself utterly alone with his own thoughts.

"I couldn't live with the guilt I felt over killing Rhonda Green," he admitted. "Even though it was an accident, the guilt was killing me. If I hadn't gone in there to rob the place; if I hadn't been so strung out on speed that I was seeing and hearing baby cops,† she'd still be alive today. I couldn't forgive myself, much less ask God's forgiveness."

"Is that what motivated you to drop all your appeals of the death sentence?" I asked.

"Yeah, partly. Besides the guilt, I was tired. Bone tired! Tired of thinking. Tired of feeling. Even tired of living. I was sick and tired of being sick and tired.

---

* A scene from a TV special about prisons broadcast by WDCN, channel 8, in Nashville in 1982.

† Speed tends to make the substance abuser increasingly paranoid. The user may, for example, end up seeing fully uniformed police officers in baby carriages.

My life has been a rat race, a clownish and morbid dance with death for as long as I can remember."

"Are you trying to commit suicide at the Governor's hand?" I asked.

He shrugged, irritated by the question. "No, " he wearily replied. "But I'm sure some people will think that. I just can't live like this any longer. My lawyers said they could keep me alive for at least 8 to 10 years. But, in the end, Ole Sparky will still be patiently waiting to hold me in her lap.

"You've lived in isolation and solitary confinement yourself, so you know how it feels. Could you have gone on like that for 10 years, knowing in the end you were going to be fried anyway?"

I had to admit I didn't know. Sensory deprivation from a prolonged stay in a solitary cell, cut off from normal communication with other people, is an acutely depressing experience that few people handle well. It's even worse for condemned prisoners on death row. With few exceptions they are universally hated and feared by other people. Their lives are empty, barren of any meaning, trivialized by a state that seeks their deaths.

Just being alive isn't enough by itself to keep people struggling with their predicament on death row. In order to be happy, condemned prisoners have to find some way to make their barren and empty existence meaningful. Ron Harries discovered that he could be happy and content, even on death row, when he discovered the secret to happiness. No matter what their circumstances, people can be happy if they have five things going for them:

1. If they have something meaningful to do.
2. If they have somebody to love.

3. If they have something to hope for.

4. If they have an attitude of thankfulness.

5. If they have a gracious God they can depend upon.

"Did God or religion mean anything to you as a kid?" I asked him.

"Nah, not really. I was baptized and confirmed as a Catholic when I was little. During reform school, and later in adult prison, I always went to the chapel services. But that was to meet friends from other blocks, make dope deals, or just get out of the cell for a couple of hours.

"I always believed in God. I just didn't want anything to do with Him. In my eyes, God was the one who was looking forward to the day He could deep-fat-fry me in the flames of hell because of my sins. God was the cosmic supercop, and I hated cops in any form!

"I was on death row for a couple of years before the ultimate questions about life, reality, and God began to rip into my consciousness. Suddenly, I realized, *I'm gonna die!* And I knew I wasn't ready to meet God and give an accounting for my life."

Samuel Johnson once dryly observed, "When a man knows he is to be hanged in a fortnight, it concentrates his mind wonderfully." Harries was beginning to concentrate for the first time in his wretched existence.

The meaninglessness and the utter destructiveness of his life tormented him every waking hour. Even though he put up a strong front for guards and other prisoners, he could see nothing but evil, depravity, and wreckage as he looked over the dreary canvas of his life. He couldn't think of his own daughter without being reminded of the teenager he'd killed. Now he wanted to do something—anything—that would give some meaning to his shabby existence. He wanted to leave something behind that would prove his life hadn't been entirely useless.

"Another death row inmate and me got this idea about working with juvenile delinquents," he said. "We called it Starting Point. The format was something like the Scared Straight program that began in New Jersey. For about six months we worked with half a dozen youngsters. And only one of 'em has been in trouble since," he added with obvious satisfaction. "I'd look into the faces of those kids," he continued, "and I saw myself 20 years ago: tough, slick, smart, and too scared to even admit I was scared and that nobody cared about me one way or the other."

He shook his head. "We took 'em to our cells on death row one day, and left 'em in there behind locked doors for about five minutes. That was a very emotional experience for them. They came out of those cells shaking!*

"I've never done much good for anybody before, but for the first time in my life I felt like I'd done something that might make a difference in a kid's life. I started this program thinking it would help the kids. When it finally ended, I realized I'd gotten the most out of it."

"How are you able to face execution by electrocution in less than a handful of days with so much patience and good humor?" I asked him. "Aren't you afraid?"

"Sure, I'm afraid. You can bet on that," he answered quietly. "Anybody who says they ain't afraid

* Warden Robert Childress, now retired, was always present with the youngsters.

of being executed is either a liar or a fool. Probably both! But I'm not afraid of dying as such. We're all gonna die someday. I'm just afraid of catching on fire like Evans did in Florida. Also, I have to admit, I'm afraid of not acting like a man at the last minute when they walk me to the chair. Getting killed is bad enough. Being humiliated at the end is even worse.

"I used to be terrified of dying and going to hell. But I can cope with all those fears now because of my faith in God. In spite of the way I've squandered my life and all the things I've done wrong, I know God still loves me and He's forgiven me. Working with those kids helped me learn something about myself. I never really cared about anybody before, including myself, until I landed on death row.

"It took me three years in this place to slow down, to stop and think. I wouldn't slow down for nothing on the streets, much less stop. Every time I got out of prison it was a mad race to catch up with all I'd missed. But I never could catch up.

"I've learned to care about people the way Kaki Warren, Jeff Blum, and Frank Bainbridge do.* They care about me, and I was able to pass some of that along to those kids. Somewhere during this whole process I began to experience God's grace and acceptance. There's nothing more to fear after that."

I sat quietly for a few minutes, remote, saying nothing, waiting for him to go on.

"Sometimes I wonder how my life might have turned out if when I was growing up as a kid I'd known

* Rev. Kaki Warren and Jeff Blum are ordained pastors active in death row and prison reform issues. Frank Bainbridge is an ordained Catholic deacon who's spent many years providing religious services and counseling for men on death row.

people like the Christians I've met while here on death row."

He shrugged. "I guess it doesn't really matter anymore. It's too late to turn back the clock for me. But maybe my story will make a difference for some of the young people who will read what you're writing about my life. I hope so."

Epilogue

Ronald Harries* came within two days of being executed. After the prison transferred Harries to the death watch cell, only a few feet away from the electric chair, a local attorney, Larry Woods, an anti-death penalty advocate, filed a brief in federal district court, asking Judge Nixon to hold (1) an evidentiary hearing on Harries' competence to make decisions for himself, and (2) a second hearing to consider what Woods alleged were the unconstitutional conditions on death row itself.

Judge Nixon ordered a stay of execution and an examination of Harries, and took the second motion under advisement. Subsequently, psychiatric experts testified that conditions on death row were so subhuman and inmates so drugged up that they couldn't make rational decisions about their own fate. Nixon found Harries incompetent and ordered other attorneys to perfect his appeal through the courts.

Harries then admitted that he didn't want to die, but he refused to do anything to further his appeals unless something was done to change the conditions on death row. Nixon ordered a hearing in which the state and prison reform advocates presented evidence

* Harries asked Governor Alexander to either commute his death sentence to life in prison without parole or sign the death warrant promptly. Governor Lamar Alexander refused to intervene in the case during 1984.

on death row conditions. It was the first time any federal court had agreed to review the constitutionality of death row conditions. Further, Judge Nixon arrived unannounced at the prison to personally review conditions on Tennessee's death row. Anybody who saw the grim-faced and tight-lipped judge as he exited from death row wasn't surprised when he later ordered sweeping changes; for example, more exercise for the men, group counseling and religious services, and a better classification system for the men. The state has fought the judge every step of the way, but he wouldn't permit them to appeal his decision until his court-appointed master could advise him the state was in compliance with his orders.

Except for Harries' unflinching willingness to die, the deplorable conditions on death row would have continued indefinitely. In a small way, Harries believes, his life now means something. He was able "to make a difference."

Tell It to
the Chaplain!

6 Cleveland Houser, D.Min., a Black Seventh-day Adventist pastor and one of four chaplains assigned to the main prison for men in Nashville, didn't know the day would end in an explosion of violence when he arrived for work at eight o'clock on the morning of July 11, 1984.

He paused briefly, after securely locking his car, and glanced up at the intimidating, gothic-style administration building. Once a great nineteenth-century mansion and nerve center for a sprawling plantation a few miles west of the city, it reminded him of a medieval castle—complete with dungeons and dragons.

"Something evil and sinister reflects off those yellow brick walls," a free world volunteer once said while trying to describe his first impressions of the prison. Prisoners have dubbed the castlelike structure Disneyland.

Houser shrugged, trying to shake off the unusual sense of apprehension as he stepped through checkpoint. It must be a fear of turning 40 tomorrow, he thought, forcing a slight smile.

Actually, he felt good about being 40. After 15 years as a pastor and university professor, the daily challenges confronting him as a prison chaplain dredged up unexpected resources of creativity which left him feeling energized and fulfilled at the end of the day.

Work detail and ball field had been called as he stepped into the trap gate that opened onto the main yard of the prison. Although early in the day, the suffocating July heat seemed trapped behind the walls. He could almost feel the human bitterness and tension radiating in the oppressive air as he watched the serpentine movement of a blue denim-clad, unsmiling mass of humanity move across the yard.

While compassionate and sympathetic toward the men he ministered to, Houser also knew the air around those men trembled with the screams of countless victims. Curiously, he was able to balance the tension between the two and minister effectively.

Mike Dutton, the recently appointed warden of the troubled institution, had moved quickly to clean up and paint the ancient, decrepit fortress. The grounds were immaculate, and the freshly watered grass sparkled in the sun. Except for the bars, uniformed guards, and all the grim faces, Houser realized that one could easily mistake the young men walking across the compound for his former students at the university.

Tension levels run high in any prison during the long, hot summer months. Prisoners and prison officials alike breathe a collective sigh of relief when the October chill chases the summer heat away for another year.

But Tennessee State Prison faced added problems that summer of 1984 when the state transferred some of the most dangerous convicts in the state to Nashville after it closed the infamous Brushy Mountain Prison in east Tennessee. The most deadly prisoners—those with a history of violent attacks on staff members and other inmates—were segregated in Unit I, the maximum security unit. But their presence aggravated the problems already present: racial conflicts, idleness, overcrowding, and general anxiety. Men who had been in the prison since the early seventies recalled what had happened the last time Brushy was closed. More than a score of men were murdered in one year.

During the last two weeks of June the prison hovered on the brink of explosion as one wild rumor after another swept through the population. Random shakedowns turned up 63 shanks, two match bombs, a .38-caliber pistol, 28 packages of marijuana, and 184 gallons of "julip"—a potent wine made from fruit. Alcohol and weapons are a deadly combination in prison, and authorities had good reason to suspect that they had confiscated only a tiny fraction of the existing contraband.

They were right.

Even though Dr. Houser continued meeting with various inmates, telling them the reports of prisoners being beaten and tortured in Unit I were utterly false, nervous inmates continued arming themselves with an impressive collection of weapons for the expected blowout.

During the same two weeks, Dr. Houser worked closely with a colleague, Elder Conn Arnold, affectionately known as "The Hoodlum's Priest" and "The Convict's Chaplain," as they prepared for a historic, month-long evangelistic series behind the walls. Nothing like that had ever been tried at the prison and inmates were curious about what the volunteer prison chaplain had in mind.

When asked for his help, Johnny Greene, an inmate leader with more than 15 years in prison, urged the 7th Step chapter to support the program. "I think this is the best thing that could happen right now," Greene said. Better than most, he knew of the danger slowly building behind the walls.

The sliding, steel-barred door rumbled open and Houser stepped out into the yard. As the door banged shut behind him, the crash of steel on steel was a blunt reminder that if a riot broke out in the prison, it was the only path to safety.

Suddenly the angry voices of a prisoner and a correctional officer interrupted his thoughts. "I don't want to hear that garbage!" the impatient officer snapped. "If you've got a problem, *tell it to the chaplain!*"

Oblivious to the chaplain's presence, two other prisoners jeered, "Yeah, tell it to the chaplain! That's as good a way to waste time as any other."

The cynical retort paints a bitter picture of an inaccurate but rigidly held belief among prisoners: *nobody,* including the chaplains, cares about their feelings or problems.

Even though he wanted to say something to the furious, tight-lipped prisoner, Houser knew that wasn't the time to interfere. Instead, he took a deep breath and walked briskly toward his office in the chapel.

It would be a long day.

Contrary to popular mythology, the majority of prisoners have little in common with the crafty and diabolical villains portrayed in the media. With few exceptions, they are young and poor. They have little education and even less self-esteem. The attitudes, values, and belief systems of the adult offenders reflect a crippling degree of arrested adolescence. What little religious orientation most received as children usually depicted God as a harsh and vindictive judge, anxious to issue a death sentence in hell for the slightest misbehavior. While most convicts believe in God, few trust Him. For the most part, they trust His chaplains even less!

Dr. Houser discovered that the behavior patterns of most felons reveal a massive capacity for self-destructiveness. And people who haven't learned to value themselves in any real sense have little capacity to care about the lives of others or their property.

Tragically, the typical state prison system only exacerbates the social and psychological problems the offender had before coming to prison. Routinely stripped of every support system considered necessary for a civilized person, and cut off from normal heterosexual and social interaction with family and friends, men in prison live in a brutal and deviant community.

"Prisons have become little more than human warehouses," James Niedergeses, Catholic bishop of Nashville, told me. "They *wear* people out!" But in an era of diminishing financial resources, however, state governments are hard pressed to include even modest educational or rehabilitative programs in their prison budgets, much less the comprehensive psychiatric treatment required for the seriously disturbed.

Oscar Wilde captured the destructiveness of prison existence on the human spirit with graphic imagery in "The Ballad of Reading Gaol."

The vilest deed like poison weeds
   Bloom well in prison-air:
It is only what is good in Man
   That wastes and withers there:
Pale Anguish keeps the heavy gate,
   And the Warden is Despair.

When hope dies in prison, as it almost always does, along with the crushed human spirit comes the wish for death. Hopelessness is the raging epidemic in any prison and violent death is all too common. Daily battles with the dragons of hopelessness and despair are the norm for the soft-spoken Black chaplain at Tennessee State Prison.

The possibility of violence in prison isn't exaggerated. But that isn't the most serious threat confronting a prison chaplain—the biggest problem is burnout. Facing the same unchanging and apparently unchangeable conditions every day, being surrounded on all sides by human rage, bitterness, and frustration, puts relentless pressure on any compassionate person.

"Frankly, I'm not concerned about burnout," Houser said after one year on the job. "When things get too bad, I keep the words of Paul in mind: 'I can do everything through him who gives me strength' [Phil. 4:13, NIV]. God doesn't call us to do more than we can—just what we can."

Preaching, prayer, and Bible study are only a part of Dr. Houser's routine. Encouraging prisoners to cultivate some sense of community, a sense of *belonging* to something and somebody else, is the major task.

"In spite of all the barbarism and inhumanity seen in a prison environment, I also get to see men going through remarkable spiritual transformations in their lives," Dr. Houser admitted. "It's a great joy to be a channel for the gospel and to baptize a convict-turned-Christian. I see the prison conditions in a different light when I focus on that.

"I can't do much to change the conditions here," he continued. "But I can help men as individuals learn how to cope with their problems through spiritual insight. A prisoner can't be free *from* prison until he is free *in* prison. That begins when he involves himself in community life and worship, when he begins playing by the rules."

Learning to be free in prison, Houser discovered, follows a process remarkably similar to the stages terminally ill patients go through in coming to terms with their own death: (1) shock; (2) denial; (3) anger; (4) self-pity, resentment, bitterness; and (5) acceptance. Usually, the prisoner experiences the stages of shock and denial in the local jail before he reaches the state penitentiary. Anger and self-pity are the most difficult stages to work through and resolve. Few men do reach the point of acceptance. A prisoner remains most dangerous to himself and others until he works out the conflicts encountered in the stages of anger and self-pity. Invariably, prisoners trapped in the acid bath of unresolved anger and self-pity commit the senseless penitentiary murders and participate in the bloody riots.

Prison is the only place in the world where people are expected to suffer the grief of loss in silence and solitude. Prisoners avoid one another when they are having problems, and the prison staff is already overworked and short of professional help. Consequently, only the chaplains are left to listen to the private anguish of a thousand men.

"It's a painful experience to tell a man his mother has died, his wife has been injured in an accident, or that his child is sick," Houser said. "And there's no easy way to do it. But God seems to have blessed me with a special kind of emotional insulation. I can listen to the pain without being overwhelmed by it. During times of crisis and suffering, I also have a chance to mediate God's grace to a man in desperate need of it."

"I appreciate Cleveland," said Amos Wilson, the senior chaplain at the prison. "He's a man of deep personal faith, a strong churchman who brings a fresh perspective to our ministry from a different religious tradition. Most important, he has the grace of one who cares deeply about others. Prisoners trust him and respond to his warmth."

"I'll tell you what I like about the man," said Vito Nappi, a convicted armed robber who has sought counsel from Dr. Houser. "He *listens!* I know he can't do anything to change my circumstances—every convict knows that. But he helps us sort things out, to get our priorities straight, by listening carefully and calling issues we might be dodging to our attention."

"Most people just want somebody to hear them, to acknowledge their feelings," Houser agreed. "Loneliness and emptiness is a heavy load to carry without some help."

"He's a man of strong principles," said Lorenzo Allen, an inmate clerk in the chaplain's office, serving 45 years for murder. "He's respected for that back here. A man might not like hearing what he says—especially if he calls something personal to their attention. But they know he cares enough about them to risk saying something. It takes guts to tell a lifer it's time for him to grow up and quit acting like a fool!

Convicts don't have much use for wishy-washy Christians. Chaplain Houser is *solid.*"

"The best way I know how to preach the gospel of Jesus Christ is to first live God's love out of my own life," Houser told me as he got ready to close his office for the day. "I don't know what's going to happen in here from one day to the next. But I do know *Who* is in control under all circumstances."

Shortly after Dr. Houser left the penitentiary on Wednesday evening, violence exploded in Unit I as 75 rampaging, maximum security prisoners broke out of their confinement and seized control of the cell block. They critically wounded one officer with multiple stab wounds and held another hostage for nearly two hours with a knife at his throat. In a frenzy of maniacal rage, prisoners demolished the cell block before heavily armed tactical officers under Warden Dutton's command regained control. Remarkably, nobody else was seriously injured and the other housing units in the prison behaved with restraint.

When Elder Arnold and other free world guests arrived for the scheduled religious services at 6:15 p.m., they saw heavily armed officers, dressed in full riot gear, racing toward the main entrance of the prison. The evangelistic crusade behind the walls appeared to be over before it really began. Incredibly, the prison resumed a normal schedule the following morning as though nothing had happened. "I'm not going to punish everybody for the violence of a few," Dutton said emphatically.

"God isn't going to let anything stop these services," Dr. Houser said. He was right. When the program ended in August, thirty men joined the Freedom Fellowship and six were baptized.

"I don't understand why you work in a place like that!" a friend told Houser recently.

He shrugged. "I guess I'd rather light a candle than curse the darkness."

A Comedy
of Grace

By Ritchie Hall

7 The sweat ran off my forehead, stinging my eyes as I chiseled away at the lock on the church office door. "This is taking too long," my partner whispered anxiously. "Let's get out of here."

"Will you relax!" I snapped irritably. I shook my head in disgust and wiped the sweat out of my eyes while I examined the door with a small penlight. "Almost finished," I grunted and went back to work, slowly demolishing the door.

Minutes later it swung open. I felt a rush of relief as I looked around, then quickly began grabbing everything of value and stuffing it into paper sacks.

"Why break into a church?" Ken* whined. "Ain't you got no respect for God at all?"

"God!" I laughed. "You've gotta be kidding. Hey, God! Are You listening up there? I'm ripping off the Lindenwood Christian church in Memphis!"

Silence.

"You want the address?" I shouted louder, doing my best Cool Hand Luke imitation.

Silence.

"See?" I said reasonably to my frightened partner.

---

* Not his real name.

"God don't care, and neither do I," I added harshly.

* * *

"You're a menace to midtown Memphis, an affliction, a one-man crime wave!" one judge said in sputtering exasperation prior to sentencing me. "You're unfit to be loose in a free, civilized society."

I agreed with him.

I was a hyperactive child. And 30 years ago nobody knew what to do with such energy. Like other children who experienced anger and ridicule under such circumstances, I cultivated a clear picture of myself early in life: "You're no good. You're bad—a liar, a thief, a cheat, a disgrace!" I heard the messages, believed them, internalized them, and behaved accordingly. A child will go to great lengths to meet negative expectations of himself.

After 25 years of criminal activity, commiting more than a thousand burglaries—as many as eight a day during the summer—and countless other acts of malicious mischief, shoplifting, and arson, it seems odd that I should remember the first theft of 30 cents from my father's pocket with such vivid clarity. I was 6 years old. With the proceeds I purchased 30 pieces of candy, sharing the chocolate with my classmates, and discovered people would like me—for a price.

Committing well-planned burglaries became an obsession with me. It was my own private war against a world that hated and despised me, a war I waged with relentless fury after I was arrested the first time at age 9 for stealing a bicycle.

One of the detectives showed me a plain looking band on his arm. "Do you know what this is?" he asked.

I shook my head.

"Every time you lie to us this thing will make my arm tingle and we'll know you're lying."

Gulping, I nodded. I'd heard of lie detectors. Quickly I confessed to several burglaries.

"What's your name, kid?" one of the detectives asked.

"Ritchie Hall."

"Oh, my arm! It's tingling again! That isn't your name."

I knew I'd been had.

* * *

On November 28, 1982, I left prison with my few possessions in a battered box and a one-way ticket to Memphis. For once I left prison with more than I had when I arrived. I had finished two years of college after a teacher explained my IQ score to me.

"Do you realize what that score says about your intelligence?" a prison counselor asked me.

"What's it worth if you don't know how to relate to other people?" I asked bitterly.

For days I wandered around Memphis, feeling disconnected and disoriented. At 28, all the loose ends of my life had come unraveled. Like Humpty Dumpty, my existence resembled a smashed eggshell. *And all the king's horses and all the king's men couldn't put Humpty together again,* I thought in utter despair.

Every time I turned on the TV, commercials for the telephone company glared at me, mocking me. "Reach out and touch someone," kept running around in my mind. I wondered if everybody except me lived in such a happy world. *Reach out and put the touch on someone is more realistic,* I thought sourly.

Time passed rapidly. As depression swept over me, I decided that either I would have to go back to prison or I had to kill myself. While I knew how to survive in the concrete jungle of a prison, I couldn't cut it in the free world.

"Quit wandering the streets and go over to the Lindenwood church," my father said. "They've got a job bank of some sort. Maybe they can even help a bum like you," he added sarcastically. "Anyway, you'd better do something quick. I don't want you around here anymore."

Lindenwood! I'd forgotten all about ripping off the church five years before. How many times did I rob them? Twice? Three times? I couldn't remember.

Desperation, more than hope, finally drove me to the church. When I walked past the office door I'd once destroyed I felt very uncomfortable. I assumed they would brush me off as soon as I told them I was an ex-con looking for work. Although I thought I was prepared for anything—including rejection—I wasn't ready for what I got: warmth, sympathy, and interest. That made me feel even more guilty. The associate pastor helped me fill out some applications and then invited me to attend the worship service. "You'll like Dr. Roy Stauffer," he said.

He was right.

Week after week I went back to the church. The reception I received from other church members was both exhilarating and terrifying at the same time. I didn't know how to deal with such open warmth and encouragement. It was totally outside the scope of my experience. Even though I committed one social faux pas after another, nobody seemed to notice. Part of me wanted to confess my burglaries of the church to Dr. Stauffer, but my mouth got dry, tasting of cotton, every time I began to bring the subject up.

I'd become a brilliant success at failure. Like every other man and woman in the criminal subculture, I knew how to cope with that dark world of criminality. There a person could cure the aching pain in the marrow of the soul with dope or booze. But I couldn't handle the success I enjoyed with those strange Christians. I knew they would despise and loathe me, too, if they knew me a little better. Even though I continued attending the church services, I drifted steadily back to the world I knew best.

The police arrested me on April 15, 1983, after catching me in the act of selling stolen diamonds to a Memphis jeweler. I didn't have the guts to kill myself, but the arrest relieved the pressure I felt in trying to deal with the Lindenwood family—and that's the way they seemed to me: *family*. I didn't know how to relate to a normal family, so I fled back into the wilderness of prison again.

* * *

When Dr. Stauffer came to visit me at the jail I expected a hostile lecture. I was ready to tell him where to go! Instead, he offered sympathy and encouragement. I received many letters and visits from him and from other members of the church. I didn't understand it at the time, but I was beginning the process of being swept up in God's grace.

On April 27, 1983, I surrendered my life to Christ.

Within weeks the prosecutor offered me a 10-year sentence as a plea bargain in exchange for dropping the habitual criminal charges, which would have meant a life sentence without parole for 30 years. Accepting the plea, I thanked God for it. Better than anybody else, I knew my sentence would stretch far into the twenty-third century if I were convicted of half the crimes I'd committed over the years.

I didn't expect to hear from Dr. Stauffer or any of his church members again after my transfer from the Memphis jail to the violence-plagued prison in Nashville. After betraying their trust and letting them down, I thought they would be glad to get rid of me. Out of sight, out of mind. However, I quickly discovered I had a lot to learn about real Christians.

As the months slowly drifted around the calendar, my volume of mail from the church kept increasing. More and more people wrote to me, and I began looking forward to their letters. Their warmth and encouragement meant a lot to me. But my burglaries of the church continued haunting me, acting as a barrier between me and deeper fellowship with the Lindenwood family.

I told my closest friend in the prison about my dilemma and asked his counsel.

Leaning back in his chair, he roared with laughter. "I love it!" he bellowed, trying to control his mirth. "All these years you've been trying to get something by breaking into the church in secret, ripping them off left and right, but now they come to you with open arms. Now that's what I call poetic justice!"

I felt more than a little miffed at his laughter. "I don't see what you think is so funny," I grumbled. "Anyway, what am I supposed to do?"

"Pick up the phone and call Roy. Get it off your chest," he said bluntly.

"They'll hate my guts and won't want anything more to do with me."

"You've got a lot to learn about the Christian life," he said softly, suddenly becoming serious. "When you get this off your chest, you're going to feel a lot better. You'll understand more about the process of forgiveness and God's grace. And Dr. Stauffer is going to have a great laugh!"

But I didn't have the courage. The weeks turned into months as I wrestled with my inner conflict. In the criminal world, there's no such thing as forgiveness, and the thought of rejection from the church family was more than I could deal with. But the guilt was worse.

God has His own time and method when it comes to leading in our lives. As the summer of 1984 drifted lazily away, three specific events helped me get mine in clearer focus.

First, my relationship with members of the Lindenwood church continued to evolve. For the first time in my life I really felt good about myself as a person. I felt worthwhile and important because I belonged to those people and they belonged to me. They trusted and respected me, and I wanted to be worthy of that confidence.

Second, I attended a month-long revival service in the prison chapel where Pastor Conn Arnold, a volunteer prison chaplain and Seventh-day Adventist Church official, was preaching. Men from many different churches attended his revival because he was so highly respected and admired.

"God is looking for a few good men behind these walls," he said on the last night. "And I want to invite you to make a public commitment of your life to Jesus

Christ." I made that public commitment, and Pastor Arnold baptized me into the Fellowship of Christ in August.

The third event began with an awareness: The realization that I didn't fit in prison anymore. I'd become a square peg in a world of round holes. Prison is a world for dying and decaying humanity, people who have little self-respect and no hope for the future. It is a world full of people alienated and estranged from God, from other people, and even from themselves. That used to be a fair description of my life, but no longer. All the violence, terror, and institutionalized insanity I once laughed at wasn't funny anymore.

While I was standing in front of a friend's cell one Friday during lunch, our conversation was interrupted by sounds of scuffling. Curious, I looked over the rail, expecting to see the usual kind of horseplay that's common among men in prison. Instead, I watched in stunned and horrified fascination as two prisoners with shanks slowly closed in on a third man.

He begged for his life, and then began screaming for help. But none came. Dozens of men stood by, laughing and joking as they watched the killing unfold. They didn't care about the victim or his attackers. It was just a noon show in the prison arena, with free admission for anybody who wanted to watch.

"Jeris, they're killing a man down there," I gasped, feeling dizzy and sick. I'd never seen anybody murdered before, but my eyes seemed locked, unable to move away from the savage drama.

One of the killers finally caught the victim from behind in a full-nelson wrestling hold, while his accomplice lunged forward with the knife, slamming it again and again into the victim's chest and abdomen, until his screams slowly died away to a grotesque, choked gurgle, and he slumped to the floor. He was fully aware of what was happening to him as he slowly died. Even after he was silent, I still saw the begging, pleading look in his eyes.

The killers stabbed and slashed the man until all three were covered in blood and the victim's head was nearly decapitated. The fingers on his right hand continued to twitch and close convulsively; then he died.

For the first time in my life I was utterly revolted by everything a penitentiary stands for. The meaningless destructiveness and hopelessness of this human zoo left me feeling drained, violated, and degraded. Staggering backward, I bumped into Jeris's cell door. I heard him talking to me quietly, urging me to put my head down and take slow, deep breaths. I felt frozen, remote and detached, unable to comprehend what I had just seen. The harsh sounds of the prison swirled around me as I gripped the cell bars for support and watched several men laughing below. A few men walked casually by the still body, carefully stepping away from the rapidly growing pool of blood. The show was over, and the bored cleanup crew came with the olive-green stretcher.

* * *

On Friday, March 1, 1985, I stopped by my friend's office in the prison chapel. "I'm going to call Dr. Stauffer and tell him about the burglaries," I said.

He grinned. "Cheer up! Quit looking like you're going to your own execution. Confession is good for the soul."

"They won't want anything more to do with me," I said gloomily.

"I doubt that very seriously," he replied. "Mark my word: Roy will be lucky if he doesn't fall out of his chair laughing. But suppose he doesn't. Suppose he hangs up on you. Does that change your responsibility to do the right thing?"

I was tempted to hang up when I heard Roy's jovial voice on the other end. But after a brief conversation, I took a deep breath and plunged in.

"I don't know how to tell you this, Roy, but I've got to confess something to you. I've put this off for a long time because I didn't want to lose your respect and friendship."

The line got very quiet. I could hear my pulse thundering in my ears and my hands were wringing wet. "What is it, Ritchie? You know I'm here to help."

"Do you remember your church being burglarized several times in the midseventies?"

"I sure do!" he emphatically replied. "We had to pay $20,000 on an alarm system to put a stop to it."

"I hate to tell you this, but I'm the one who did it. I don't even remember how many times, but I think it was three or four."

The line crackled with silence. I waited for the slamming noise of the receiver. But he burst out laughing! Was he laughing at me? I felt stunned.

"I'm not laughing about the burglaries," he said, trying to catch his breath. "But this is a wonderful, priceless story about God's grace."

I felt dazed and light-headed after talking to him. It was the first time in my life I'd *ever* confessed any wrongdoing to another person, and I couldn't believe he'd forgiven me so easily. When I returned to my friend's office, he looked at me and grinned.

"He laughed! He roared with laughter, just like you said he would," I mumbled in astonishment. "It's all over. I don't deserve it, but he's forgiven me and says his church will, too."

"Do you remember asking me to define grace for you a couple of months ago?" Jeris asked.

I nodded.

"You've just discovered the comedy of God's grace, encountering a large dose of it radiating off Roy Stauffer. Now, go thou and do likewise," he added in mock severity.

I was beginning to understand.

Straight
Ahead

8 The typical maximum-security prison is a seething caldron of human rage. The physical and social environment is a corrosive, acid bath of bitterness, hatred, and despair. Jack Henry Abbott, the controversial convict author, has described imprisonment in the American prison system as analogous to existence "in the belly of the beast."

In spite of superficial appearances to the contrary, the state prison in Nashville, Tennessee, contains the same deadly, destructive characteristics of such infamous prisons at Attica and New Mexico where scores of prisoners died during bloody rioting in recent years.

Addressing a local Rotary Club meeting November, 1983, Judge Ernest Pellegrin, newly appointed commissioner of correction, described the prison system over which he presides as a "cesspool of hate."

He wasn't exaggerating. I know—I live in that cesspool.

Dozens of men have been murdered behind these walls during the nine years I've been incarcerated. Scores have been stabbed with shanks (homemade knives, usually measuring between 5 and 10 inches in length) manufactured in the prison metal shop. Hundreds have been robbed, beaten, raped, sodomized, or victimized by an ingenious variety of prisoner-run extortion and protection rackets.

After a decade of protracted litigation, federal district Judge L. Clure Morton issued a blistering opinion on August 11, 1982, declaring in brutally frank language that incarceration in the state's beleaguered prison amounted to "cruel and unusual punishment." Saying that inmates lived in an environment "where violence and terror reign," he went on to describe some prison housing as little more than "human cages unfit for human habitation."

It is to this deviant and violent subculture that Elder Conn Arnold, then director of personal ministeries for the Kentucky-Tennessee Conference, began his unique prison ministry on July 19, 1980.

* * *

While few prison officials will acknowledge it publicly, every convict population has its own subterranean power structure and cadre of inmate leaders. Any prison is a small town, and it cannot be ruled without the consent or the assistance of the governed.

A small handful of men set the pace in any prison, basing their power upon subtle, difficult to define qualities. Their influence is their power, and the roots of both are sunk deep in the concrete of the convict code, not threats of violence as the free world commonly believes.

Such men have the respect of their peers. They are the ones who make things happen behind the walls. During times of unrest and tension their leadership—

or thunderous silence—can restrain violence or allow pent-up forces to explode in bloody mayhem.

Convict leaders also determine which free world people are entitled to trust and that elusive, critically important quality in prison known as respect. They don't tell anybody else what to do or who to trust—they lead by personal example.

Most prisoners view free world "religious" people with enormous distrust. Their presence in any penitentiary is tolerated with bemused, wry humor, but the inmates don't take them seriously. Until Arnold began his involvement with the Nashville prison, no prison ministry had ever effectively penetrated that gray, nebulous world of the convict power structure.

Typically, prison officials like free world volunteers and prisoners despise them. Others the prisoners will like, but the prison administration will distrust. Elder Arnold quickly earned the respect, trust, and admiration of both.

"He is an exceptional man for any denomination," said Amos L. Wilson, chief of chaplaincy services for the state prison system. "He brings a lot of energy, ethics, and interest to this work. People intuitively sense his integrity. Few people have his capacity to relate to such a broad spectrum of men in prison who otherwise rarely relate to church people."

Elder Arnold seemed attracted to the toughest characters in the prison. Since most of them wouldn't be caught dead in the chapel, he went out looking for them, readily joining the inmate clubs, attending their social functions, and laughing good naturedly when prisoners teased him a bit.

"I just don't know how to introduce our speaker tonight," an inmate said the first time Arnold appeared at a 7th Step meeting. "You all know him by now. He's been out here to visit regularly. In fact, I heard that Warden Vandever was going to give him a prison number since he's around here all the time. Even so, I feel strange introducing a Seventh-day Adventist Church official to a bunch of convicts when his first name is *Conn!*"

The dining room exploded in laughter.

By 1982 Elder Arnold received official credentials as a volunteer chaplain. He was the only church official allowed unlimited access to any part of the prison. At least once every couple of weeks he made a tour, chatting with men in the cell blocks, visiting with them in the disciplinary unit or at the hospital. It could take him 30 minutes to move 30 yards when the compound was crowded with men. Everybody wanted to shake his hand and say Hello.

"There's something seriously wrong with a man who don't feel good after being with Conn for a few minutes," said Larry Carter, an inmate worker at the laundry who regularly attends the Adventist chapel programs. "He *makes* men feel good about themselves."

"I'll bet I've heard him say 'Straight ahead!' a hundred times," another prisoner admitted.

"That's my philosophy about life," Arnold explained during a talk with a group of inmates. "I'm not here to preach you got what you deserved—I'm here to preach you *didn't* get what you've got coming from God. And that's *freedom, joy* and *fulfillment!* Don't be a slave to your present circumstances. Pick up the pieces of your life and begin again. Now! Today!

"God has a plan for your life *now!* Never mind the past. God has forgiven you. Ignore what's on your left or to the right, you'll only be distracted.

"Straight ahead!"

* * *

Edward "Rick" Bettner, 39, was one of those incorrigible prisoners Conn sought out. After more than 20 years of incarceration in some of America's most deadly prisons, Rick was a highly skilled, predatory human tiger who could take care of himself. He took great pride in the grim reputation he enjoyed as one of the prison's most ruthless and violent dope dealers: a man who wouldn't think twice about working another man over with a baseball bat for not paying his dope bill on time.

But Rick's world turned upside down when he began attending Elder Arnold's month-long revival held in the prison chapel during July and August. When the minister made a call for repentance and a commitment to Jesus Christ, saying, "God needs a few good men behind these wall," other prisoners were visibly stunned when Bettner responded.

"I don't know what you're up to, but don't you be making fun of that man [Conn Arnold]," one prisoner growled ominously.

People were even more startled during the following weeks as Rick went to every man he'd ever offended in the prison—and was it a long list!—and asked their forgiveness. "I've asked Conn to baptize me soon," he said, "and I want to make things right with people."

Like the apostle Paul, who also met hostile skepticism immediately after his dramatic Damascus road encounter, Rick soon learned how distrustful people were of his confession of faith.

"You're just trying to trick people," one convict told him bluntly.

"While I do believe in the sincerity of faith, I have to admit you're the last man on earth I would have expected to become a Christian," I told him one day during lunch. "What happened to you during those services?"

"I thought it would be funny for somebody like me to be going to church," he admitted quietly. "You know what a smart aleck I can be. I'd sit there in the pew, looking around at people, smirking, putting the make on the free world women, and thinking everybody in the chapel was a weak punk for buying into all that religious garbage.

"But back in my cell, when I was alone with myself and the mirror one night, I suddenly realized I was the weak punk—and a stupid one at that! I can't think of a serious crime in the book I haven't committed at least once. I'm serving two life sentences for kidnapping and bank robbery, and I was proud of that."

He paused a moment, looking deeply within for words.

"I've watched Conn out here over the past few years, and I knew everybody loved the man. There are convicts in here who don't like anybody else on the face of this earth, but they think he's the greatest thing since sliced bread! They look up to him, admire him, trust him, and they like being around him.

"And then I had to look at myself. Talk about a depressing experience! I'm nearly 40, and I had to admit my life added up to a big, fat zilch! Nobody even liked me, much less loved me. Nobody respected me or looked up to me. Nobody wanted to be around me. If I were to suddenly drop dead, I knew everybody who knew me would cheer."

He shook his head. The usually glib and articulate prisoner was at a loss of words.

"I can remember laughing at 'Murph the Surf' when we did time together in the Florida pen. I thought he was running a slick con on the whole world, but I was a fool. As I listened to Conn preach, I knew I had to have what he and Murph had in their lives. When I finally realized it was *Who* they had—Jesus Christ—I surrendered my life to Him on the spot."

Like the prodigal son in Jesus' parable, Rick "came to his senses." (Luke 15:17, NIV). All the energy and creativity he once invested in the penitentiary rackets he rechanneled into witnessing for Christ. "Don't even bother asking Rick for something to get high on anymore," a former drug customer grumbled. "He'll hand you a Bible!"

In August 1984 Bettner stepped into the baptismal tank in the prison chapel and was baptized by the convict's chaplain: Elder Conn Arnold.

Rick stopped by my office on November 15, 1984, to talk with me about a tape we were going to make the following day for students at Georgia-Cumberland Academy. He had a growing passion to do something concrete about his faith, and he looked forward to giving his testimony to those students.

"I'll be getting out next month, Jeris," he said as we went our separate ways. "I'm going to devote the rest of my life to some kind of a prison ministry. Maybe I can help pay Conn back for all he's done for me and all the rest of us back here. Straight ahead, Jeris!" he laughed.

Those were the last words I heard from Rick.

Within hours an old adversary crept up behind him while he stood in front of his cell door. As Rick turned to his right, the shank flashed through the air, sinking deep into his back. Momentarily stunned, he whirled around and knocked his assailent to the floor. He tried to get away, but other prisoners blocked his path, some of them beginning to scream and chant.

"Kill the snitch! Kill that punk! Cut his head off! Throw 'em off the walk!"

I could hear the demonic screams from my cell, a familiar penitentiary sound that meant there was another killing. The same spirit that motivated other men to scream, "Crucify Him! Crucify Him!" was still alive and well.

Guards tried to push through the mob to rescue the wounded prisoner, but other inmates casually obstructed their path, tripping one of the officers on the stairs.

With furious determination Rick's attacker closed in for the kill, coming at him again and again, ripping and slashing the mortally wounded man's arms to bloody ribbons until he finished him off with two final stab wounds to the chest.

Rick Bettner died 20 minutes later in the prison chapel.

The killing stunned the convict population. The next day men gathered in small groups and tried to make some sense of the murder. "He lived the life of a fool for 39 years and never got hurt," one man said. "He becomes a Christian and gets killed two months later. That don't make no sense!"

"I think God knew what was coming and got him ready for it," Larry Carter suggested.

That night the Adventist Freedom Fellowship

turned the usual Bible study hour over to a memorial service for Rick. It was the first such service ever held in the prison for a murdered fellow prisoner. Many of the men who rarely attended came inside the chapel.

Elder Arnold talked quietly and reflectively about the uncertainty of life. "But this isn't the last word about Rick," he said firmly. "The Christian has eternity to look forward to with great joy."

He glanced out over the blue-denim-clad congregation and the familiar words echoed through the chapel: "Straight ahead, men! Straight ahead!"

They Said It Couldn't Be Done

*9*When the police narcotics squads crack down on drug traffic, all the junkies begin to panic as the supply of dope dwindles and the prices leap through the roof. Billy Smith, 28, a drug addict for half his life, decided to relieve the raw, aching hunger for a fix by robbing a drugstore in Knoxville, two days before Valentine's Day in 1980.

His stomach felt like it was tied in throbbing knots as he eased the car into a parking slot in front of the store. The gut-wrenching cramps almost doubled him over. His first armed robbery.

He played the role of a pharmaceutical salesman. The harried druggist barely looked past the conservative three-piece suit and professional briefcase carried by the clean-cut young man before waving him toward the office in the back of the store.

Once alone with the man, Smith dropped the strained smile. Cold sweat broke out on his face as he reached for the pistol in the briefcase. "This is a robbery! I want all your narcotics!" he croaked. His voice sounded hollow and far away. The 10 blue Valium he'd ingested 20 minutes before suddenly hit him, and his legs began feeling rubbery.

The frightened druggist never got a chance to

answer the thief. Smith's hands started shaking uncontrollably. Instinctively, he stiffened to conceal his fear. The pistol roared and a bullet exploded harmlessly into the ceiling. The terrified druggist bolted through an open door into the back alley.

Billy felt like he was floating. Drunkenly, he stumbled back into the drugstore. People screamed and ducked for cover when they saw the pistol. He tripped over something, smashing headlong into a display counter. The pistol barked again. A strange burning sensation bit savagely at his thigh. He didn't realize he'd shot himself. Everything seemed to be flowing in slow motion as he staggered through the front door and hobbled over to his car.

The streetlights assaulted his eyes, blinding him as he sped erratically down the street. His mouth tasted of dry cotton balls. A police helicopter spotted the car when he sideswiped another vehicle. Within minutes he was in police custody—the end of a short-lived career as an armed robber.

* * *

His eyes snapped open. A gut-wrenching terror seized him as screaming voices and the reverberating crash of steel doors smashing on steel tore through his soggy consciousness.

"Happy Valentine's Day!"

He started to roll over on his right elbow to peer at the sarcastic, disembodied voice. But the blaze of a thousand popping flash bulbs slashed through his bleary eyes from the throbbing pain in his right leg. Slumping back, he tried to collect his drug-befuddled wits. The disembodied voice could wait. Ragged fragments of the past two days chewed on the edge of his memory like little mice after cheese. Jail! He knew he was in jail, but couldn't remember why.

The front door of jail wasn't a stranger to him. Robbery, drugs, larceny, burglary, stolen property— you name it and he'd done it several times. The jail door was a revolving one for him. In and out, and back in again. Faster and faster.

Slowly he pulled himself up into a sitting position again on the steel bunk, staring silently at the ugly gunshot wound in his right thigh. Vaguely he remembered shooting himself while racing away from the drugstore.

"Smith!" The jailer stood in front of the cell door, looking impassively at the prisoner.

"What am I doing here?" Billy muttered. His tongue felt thick, dry, and dead as he stumbled to his feet.

"You'll find out," the jailer answered.

Ten minutes later he realized he didn't have any shoes on as he stood in front of the booking officer. "Armed robbery. Possession of drugs for resale. Leaving the scene of an accident." Mechanically, the man read off the list of charges. Bored. He wasn't even angry—just bored. Billy felt like an insect, pinned alive, wriggling on a specimen board. He kept staring at his bare feet.

Back in the cell, he lay quietly on the bunk, trying to avoid thinking about the pain in his leg. The list of criminal charges bounced around in his mind like marbles in a tin can. He knew he was looking at a life sentence. *Why not?* he thought sourly. *I've been doing a life sentence on the installment plan for half my life.*

Then the chills began, and the bile replaced his

sour laughter. The muscle spasms in his stomach seized him, shaking him like a dog worrying a bone. Dope is a vicious master, cold, heartless, and diabolical. A junkie would sell his mother into white slavery for a fix. "You're a junkie, a sack of human garbage!" his mind kept screaming.

Other memories slashed through his thoughts. "This is my little preacher boy," his grandmother had once said proudly as she held him on her knee. "Jesus loves you, and you're going to grow up to be His mighty soldier!" she promised.

So much for that promise!

How did my life get so messed up? he wondered. *What am I doing here? What's wrong with me? Why can't I pull myself together?* He had all the right questions, but no answers.

Church had been fun when he was a kid. But somewhere—and he honestly didn't remember when, why, or how—it turned into a drudgery. Wanting to be like his friends, he began smoking and drinking, and gradually drifted into drug addiction. One day he woke up and realized he was hooked like a fish.

"Billy, please straighten up and come back to church with your dad and me," his mother had pleaded so often.

"Ah, lemme alone, Ma. I know what I'm doing!" he growled. A real tough guy. He had worlds to conquer and he didn't need any advice from his mother.

The pain in his gut doubled him up on the bunk. The memories vanished like vapor under a hot sun, and he felt his life draining out of him. The sweat trickled off his forehead, soaking the dingy pillow under his head.

"Smith!"

Startled, he sat up on the bunk too quickly and smashed his head into the top bunk. "Get up!" the guard barked. "You've got a visitor."

As he stumbled down the long hall toward the visiting booth, each step sent waves of nausea and pain through him. Slumping down on the steel stool, solidly bolted into the concrete floor, he looked through the thick bulletproof glass at his wife on the other side. He hadn't seen her or talked to her in several weeks.

She picked up the phone on her side of the glass. "They told me what happened, Billy," she said softly. "How? Why?"

How and why, indeed! He fumbled for words, trying to explain something he really didn't understand himself. Like most junkies he used drugs to deaden an existential anguish and pain he couldn't describe. That pain is a malignant cancer which requires more and more dope to anesthetize the pain.

"God loves you, Billy. And so do I," she said when he finally ran out of words. Timidly, she began telling him about Jesus' love. He wanted to scream at her, "Shut up! I've heard it all before!" But he was too exhausted to protest. And a curious part of him was listening.

"Time's up, Smith!" a voice barked. Even a whisper seemed like a roar. Tears filled the eyes of his young wife as they each hung up the phone. As she turned and walked away, tears began running down his face. His only contact with sanity was walking away. She turned once, blew him a kiss from her fingertips, and mouthed the words, "I love you, Billy."

Back in the cell, huddled in a corner, with his back braced against the wall, he continued to wrestle with the pain that throbbed through his body. It was a raw, aching pain that bit into him with steel teeth. It was more than withdrawal—guilt was chewing him up. Every miserable, sordid deed he'd ever committed flashed through his mind, lashing out angrily at the gentle words of love from his wife. How could she love him after all the abuse he'd inflicted on her? How could God forgive him for all the crimes he'd committed?

More questions. No answers.

Without realizing how it began or what he was doing, he found himself praying. He didn't know what to say or how to say it. He just knew he had to pray. When a man was as far down as he was, he had only two alternatives left: either commit suicide or begin the long, slow crawl up out of the sewer. When stretched to the furthest limit, many people respond with faith.

"Lord, please help me," he began. "I want what my wife's got. If it's real, I want it!" Time and space drifted away, and for a long time he poured out all the words about his life to God. There weren't any sudden explosions or revelations of ecstasy. Instead, he felt a gentle, reassuring peace beginning to flow over him. He wasn't hurting anymore. Inside or out. His muscles were sore from the cramps, but the withdrawal pain had vanished.

In the words of his wife, he had encountered God's love and grace. Through her he experienced God's nonnegotiable forgiveness and acceptance. "It's real!" he whispered in awe as the tears began running down his cheeks again.

"Hey, Rap; you all right?"

He looked at the two men in the cell. They were watching him anxiously. His face flushed as he realized what they were probably thinking. When he tried to share what had happened to him with them, their fear quickly turned to laughter. Then he laughed, too, and laid back on the bunk.

"Finally, I do know what I'm doing, Mom. I'll be all right," he whispered under his breath.

* * *

Ten months later, just before Christmas, manacled in clanking belly chains and leg irons, Smith rode the prison bus through the gates of Brushy Mountain State Prison in Petros, Tennessee, to begin serving an 18-year term. "Perish all hope, ye who enter these gates," the bus driver called out cheerfully.

Very funny.

Brushy is an ominous, fortress-style prison built right into the side of Brushy Mountain. For years the threat of being shipped to Brushy for punishment— an end-of-the-line death trap reserved for the most dangerous convicts—has struck terror into the hearts of the most hardened criminal.

Nobody escapes from Brushy, at least not alive. "We got extra UN-O-FISH-UL guards around here," a stone-faced officer coldly told Billy. "Timber rattlers. The mountains are infested with 'em."

He wasn't kidding. Every day they fell off the back wall and slithered around on the open prison yard. But Bill shrugged philosophically. He'd never felt better in his life, and he had no interest in escaping. After experiencing the phenomenon of being born again in jail, and being liberated from the despair of drug addiction, Brushy seemed fairly tame to him.

"Where's the chapel?" he asked a passing prisoner

shortly after arriving.

"Chapel!" The man spat in disgust. "Are you one of those Bible-totin' sissies? There ain't no chapel in this zoo. Hey, Rap," he called to another convict. "This fool wants to know where the chapel is!"

The cellblock exploded in jeers, catcalls, and derisive laughter. "Des da widdow boy want his mommy, too?" somebody taunted scornfully.

"Nah, he's looking for a daddy!" somebody shouted.

Billy shrugged again.

It didn't take long to find all the Christians or the chapel. Brushy had a grand total of seven—eight, counting Billy—and the chapel services met Sunday morning in the same auditorium where some of the most vile X-rated films ever produced were shown every Saturday night. The pathetically small band of Christians wanted a chapel. Everybody said it couldn't be done, but Billy decided it was time to talk to the warden about getting one.

* * *

Warden Herman Davis was a poker-faced, middle-aged man who stood six feet four and weighed in at a solid 200 pounds.

"Good morning, Warden," Billy said as Davis walked past him one day in the chow hall. "I'd like to talk to you about building a chapel here behind the walls."

The temperature in the room suddenly dropped as the warden turned and fixed Smith with a stony, expressionless stare. "Do you see the top of that mountain?" he finally asked, pointing toward the peak of Brushy Mountain.

Billy nodded.

"That's where God stops and I begin. I'm the *only* god on Brushy Mountain." He walked away without another word.

The summer began on a grim note. Racial tensions mounted and extortion and protection rackets flourished openly. Some prisoners being victimized or threatened, retaliated in violent rage, striking out at one another in deadly ferocity. The dream of buildng a chapel behind the walls seemed more and more absurd.

"O God," Billy prayed, "My brothers here need a special place to worship you. We'll build it with our own hands if You will make it possible."

The following day the smoldering human cauldron at Brushy erupted in violence that made national headlines. James Earl Ray, the state's most infamous prisoner, convicted of assassinating civil rights leader Dr. Martin Luther King, Jr., walked into the library. After 13 years of relative safety, Ray felt no alarm.

Four shank-wielding Blacks, waiting in ambush, surrounded the slightly built and graying man. Blocking his exit and closing in for the kill, they slashed and stabbed him repeatedly until he was nearly dead.

Ray survived the attack, and security got even tighter. Nothing moved inside the prison. Several of the recently converted Christians gave up in discouragement. Hopes for a chapel appeared to be more futile than ever in the midst of the rising tide of violence.

In July, Billy Edmans, a local pastor, told Smith a man in his congregation had made $10,000 available for any project of his choice. "If I can get you the materials, can you men build the chapel?" Edmans asked.

Bill smiled ruefully. "Give me some blueprints and material, and I can build anything. But we don't have a place to build."

Even though months of prayer didn't appear to have accomplished anything for the fledgling Christian community behind the walls, the resistance and endless obstacles just made the men more determined. They turned up the voltage on their prayers.

Defeat can be a valuable emotional experience for people who refuse to accept it as the final word. In the emptiness of that human wasteland, where convicts are the most powerless people on earth, these men had a dream they refused to let die. They turned to God and prayed some more.

Within days Warden Davis received a directive from Nashville, ordering him to make space available for a chapel. "You can have your chapel in the old library," Davis said. "You build it yourselves!" he added with emphatic contempt.

Over the years scores of men had died in that dingy building. For decades before being converted into a library, the same space had been used as "the hole": blacked-out strip cells where men lived for months without light, running water, clothes, blankets, or a bunk to sleep on. They used a hole in the floor for body wastes. Many strong men went mad in the darkness.

Was the space set aside as a cynical gesture? Billy didn't know or care. But he did love the obvious symbolism. What better choice for a prison chapel than the place where so many men had been tortured, broken, and murdered. Billy drove the first nail the week before Thanksgiving in 1981.

The prisoners dedicated Christ Chapel on February 7, 1982. In a final gesture of defiant optimism, they placed the rustic-style pulpit over the exact spot where Ray was nearly murdered only months before.

During the first formal worship service the prison exploded in another frenzy of racial violence which sent political shockwaves throughout the state. Seven White prisoners seized guards at gunpoint in B Block and held them hostage while two other men systematically hunted down four Black prisoners, summarily executing two of them on the spot and critically wounding the other two.

While the prison hovered precariously on the brink of a massive disaster, more and more convicts found their way to Christ Chapel, the only place where Whites and Blacks could meet without weapons. While police officials swarmed like angry bees throughout the institution, trying to find out who was providing prisoners with pistols, the musical strains of men singing "Amazing Grace" drifted across the prison compound.

"It's hard to talk about the feelings I had that day," Billy told me. "Just two years before I was shooting dope and killing myself on the installment plan. But for the first time in my life I did *something*, contributed *something* to life that matters. A lot of men have found Christ in that chapel during the last couple of years. Working to build that chapel was my way of 'passing it on.' "

Author's Note: Shortly after the dedication of the chapel, Billy was transferred to the main prison in

Nashville, and Brushy was closed as a maximum-security prison. He became an active supporter of the Adventist Freedom Fellowship behind the walls.

A Peculiar Coincidence

By Edward C. Ley

10 I hunched my shoulders and pulled my coat a little tighter against the late afternoon chill. Usually I'm not one for drifting too long in a gloomy mood, but the pressures were getting under my skin. The emotional contamination from working for many years in the criminal subculture can be exhausting.

It seemed as though I spent most of my time shoveling sand against a relentless tide. At least that's the way I felt last December as I left the university and began walking the few blocks between the campus and the county jail. I wondered if I was beginning to skate on the thin edge of burnout.

Exams had ended for the semester and I was that much closer to finishing my master's degree in criminal justice. I tried to generate a feeling of accomplishment as the six-story criminal justice building came into sight. The effort was wasted.

I wear two hats at the jail. One has a badge—I'm a probation officer with the state prison system. The second hat also has a badge of sorts—a cross. I preach at the jail each Sabbath evening for approximately 30 prisoners who attend the service. In addition, I also provide personal counseling during times of crisis.

The two hats have at least one common denomina-

tor, I thought sourly. I spend most of my time filling out forms, listening to tragic stories about ruined lives, and wondering if I'm accomplishing anything by all the time and energy spent on the job.

I began to pray. "Lord, give me guidance . . . "

Suddenly a young man standing directly in front of me on the sidewalk interrupted my concentration. I almost ran into him before he stepped out of the way.

"Mister, I hate to bother you, but could you spare 67 cents so I can get something to eat at the church soup kitchen?"

My first thought was to brush him off. I didn't have much money anyway, and I had more important things to think about. But something held me back. There's an aura around some ex-cons that stands out like a flashing light. After a few years of working the streets as a cop and a probation officer, my sixth sense tunes in on that signal like radar.

"I just got out of prison six months ago," he blurted out, perhaps sensing my hesitation, "and I'm having a tough time finding steady work."

"Were you at the Walls?"

"Yeah, I spent five years in that lunatic asylum!" he answered emphatically.

"I was just going to visit somebody at the jail, but I'm hungry myself. Come with me and we'll have lunch at the cafeteria." .

Now he hesitated.

"I work at the jail in my church's prison ministry," I added. "Maybe you can tell me a little more about life at the state prison. How's that for a fair trade?"

As soon as the words were out of my mouth I inwardly kicked myself for the impetuous gesture. But it was too late to back out. I almost said something about being a probation officer, but ex-cons tend to be more than a little wary around people who carry badges. Deciding he didn't need to know, I made a mental note to remember which hat I was wearing.

Once we were seated at our table, Allen* began telling me about his life. It was a painfully familiar story, a broken record that I've heard too many times from other convicts and juveniles I work with. He knew more about the state criminal code than most lawyers.

"I'm 28 now," he said quietly, "and I'm finished with all that. I'm just lucky I never caught a murder rap. I came just that close several times," he added, holding up his right thumb and forefinger less than an inch apart.

"Did the five years in prison finally do the trick?" I mechanically asked, only half listening to him.

"No, it wasn't the time. Doing time is the thing I know best," he ruefully admitted. "I've been locked up so long and so often it don't even bother me anymore after the first few weeks."

"What's so different for you now?"

"I was strung out on drugs when I got sent up last time and I stayed that way in the joint. My wife came up to see me one day, and she said something about the kids needing a father. She wasn't nagging me—just telling me the plain truth. And for the first time in my life I felt like a low-life critter.

"When it came time for her to leave, I knew I wouldn't be seeing her again. Yet I couldn't get what she said out of my mind. I got so depressed after a couple of weeks I was ready to cut it short." †

* Not his real name.
† Commit suicide.

He started to light a cigarette, but stopped. I noticed his hands were shaking from the tension of remembering something deeply disturbing. I looked at him a little more closely.

"I don't want to pry into your life if you don't want to talk about it," I said quickly. "But I must admit I am curious about what happened to change your mind."

"That's OK. You're easy to talk to," he replied, poking thoughtfully at his pie with a fork and staring off into deep space.

"I had a cell partner. He used to be just like me, only worse. He's spent so much time locked up he used to tell people he was born at the women's prison! Then he got involved with some straight-up cons in the 7th Step program behind the walls. That's a convict-run group for hardcore incorrigible types who want to get their lives straightened out."

"I know the group quite well," I admitted.

"Anyway, after a while he quit shooting dope and running all over the joint like a fool. He even started going to church!" Allen shook his head at the wonder of that, and looked embarrassed when I smiled at him.

"I don't mean anything bad by that, Preacher. I started going to church myself not too long ago. But him going to the prison chapel was far out!"

I felt the excitement beginning to rise within me. Before he finished the story, I knew it was an answer to my half-finished prayer of less than an hour before.

He shrugged. "I guess there isn't much else to tell. I went to one remotivation class feeling lower than a snake's belly, but I ended up getting hooked on something better than any dope: self-respect.

"The first day I was there this convict who ran the class was telling a story about a baby eagle that was

116

captured by a farmer and raised with his chickens. The eagle believed he was a chicken, so he couldn't fly. He didn't even try—just spent his life scratching around in the dirt like the other chickens.

"One day, a naturalist came by and took the eagle up to a high mountain where he taught him to fly by telling him over and over again, 'You're an eagle, not a chicken. Stretch forth your wings and fly.'

"When he finished telling the story, he looked me right dead in the eye and said, 'Maybe you grew up thinking like a chicken, but God gave you the heart of an eagle, too. Now you stretch forth your wings and fly!'

"For the next few weeks the class centered around getting high on life instead of dope. The dude who ran the class said, 'Good friends are the most natural high in the world.' One day he told the whole class that his best friend was a Christian and an ex-cop now working as a probation officer for the state."

Allen shook his head at the audacity of such an admission.

"That room got so quiet you could hear people think! I'm here to tell you not many cons would have the guts to tell a group of prisoners that his best friend packs a badge. That's a great way to get isolated real quick."

I felt my eyes beginning to sting.

"That was nearly two years ago and I haven't touched a lick of dope since. It was hard changing some of those old habit patterns, but that dude kept telling me, 'It takes guts to get out of the ruts!' "

He cleared his throat several times, then drank a glass of water before he could go on.

"I went to his class for nearly a year, but I never did

tell him how much he helped change my life. He paused and then chuckled.

"What's so funny?" I asked.

"I was thinking about the friendship between those two men. One's a cop and the other is a con doing a life sentence. You must admit that's an unlikely combination. I'd like to meet that cop and find out what he's all about. He probably doesn't even know how much encouragement he's given to his friend or how his friend has passed it on to other cons."

"Yes, that does sound like an unusual friendship," I admitted as I reached into my pocket and pulled out my credentials for Allen to look at.

At first he looked frightened, then confused. "You're that cop! You know this guy?" He was flabbergasted.

"Yes, I know him well. We've been friends for many years. Just before I ran into you this afternoon, I was wondering what on earth I was doing in this line of work. You just reminded me that things aren't always as they appear on the surface."

My step was lighter as I left the restaurant and walked the last few blocks to the jail. As I thought about the unexpected encounter with Allen, I remembered a line in one of Jack's* letters to me. "It's hard to tell about a coincidence," he wrote. "Sometimes a coincidence is just God performing a miracle when He wants to remain anonymous."

Obviously, we all need to know that our work is meaningful, that our efforts do matter. But it is equally important to know—if only by faith—that God takes our work and makes more out of it than we could have

* Not his real name.

imagined.

I was ready to go back to work with some real enthusiasm.

My Mother Lived God's Grace

11 "Many people speak of God exclusively in terms of male imagery," Valerie said. "But your metaphors are both masculine and feminine, usually portraying God in the most warm, gracious, and loving terms. Where did your ideas about God come from?"

Her question startled me. I'd never given any serious thought about where my vision of God originated, much less the subtle distinctions between gender imagery.

"You're beginning to sound like Barbara Walters, suddenly asking questions from out in left field," I teased the young radio announcer from WSMC-FM. "Anyway, I thought you wanted to interview me about prison ministry."

"I want that, too, but right now I want to know whether your mother or father most influenced the way you think about God."

I tried giving her a neatly worded theological answer, using examples of God's grace from both the Old and New Testaments: Jacob, David, Rahab, Hosea and Gomer, Mary Magdalene, Peter, and Paul. What I said was true, but I knew something even more fundamental was truer. An old memory nudged me, but it wouldn't quite come into focus.

"Some people might read your magazine articles and suspect you of promoting cheap grace," she said, pressing her question further. "In any event, you're giving me a complicated, abstract, intellectual answer when I asked you for a personal one."

Grace isn't cheap—it's free," I peevishly replied, irritated by that old buzz phrase. "God's grace is costly only to God. That grace can never be exaggerated, regardless of gender metaphors used to describe the phenomenon."

She grinned and I realized I'd come very close to being sarcastic with her. "You certainly have some very strong feelings attached to what you believe about God," she said, still smiling, "but that still doesn't tell me what your thinking is rooted in."

I looked at the quiet and reserved college woman with new interest. Clearly, she didn't intend to settle for a casual answer. Her tenacity reminded me of somebody I once knew, but the image was fuzzy. Then I remembered.

"You're 21 or 22, aren't you?" I abruptly asked.

"Twenty-one," she replied, puzzled by such a disconnected question. "Why do you ask?"

"I was just thinking about my mother when she was your age," I said as my memory sowly wandered back over the twists and turns of three decades.

My 5-year-old world shattered when my father, a gentle and loving man of 22, suddenly suffered a devastating series of strokes and heart attacks that left him partially paralyzed on his left side and unable to speak intelligibly for many months.

My mother, a high school dropout who married at 16, was barely out of her teens when she finally brought him home from the hospital. He looked ghastly. The once tall and handsome man seemed withered, pale, and his face was covered with a grizzled beard that exaggerated the dazed expression on his face. Looking at me without recognition, he struggled to say something. But the sounds were an incoherent babble.

I ran away and hid in the dark security of the toolshed for several hours, wondering why God would allow my father to be so desperately sick.

As the months slowly passed, I watched my mother patiently caring for him: feeding and dressing him; constantly changing and washing the soiled bed sheets; talking to him and encouraging him to exercise. Over the door frame in the kitchen she hung a pulley contraption with clothesline rope threaded through the pulley and two handles on each end of the rope. His lifeless left hand hung limply over one handle while he pulled on the other with his right hand. Up and down went his arms, hour after hour, while the squeaking of the pulley echoed through the house and he stared off into some dark and empty space of his own.

The man who once swept me up over his head, carrying me lightly on his shoulders, wasn't strong enough to even grip the pulley with his left hand. That pulley was an enigmatic riddle to me. I pulled on each end of the rope with both hands, wondering what there was about the exercise that was good for my father.

And then my mother encouraged him to walk again.

He lost his balance easily and fell awkwardly to the floor the first time she let him walk without leaning on her arm. His eyes looked wild with fear and his arms

123

and legs drew up defensively into a fetal position. For a brief moment he reminded me of a peculiarly shaped turtle on its back with arms and legs sprawling aimlessly and helplessly in the air.

I burst out laughing at the strange sight.

She helped him get up and stumble back to his chair. Then she took my hand and firmly led me into the kitchen and sat me on the table. I was more stunned than hurt when her right hand shot out and lightly smacked me in the face. It's the only time she ever slapped my face and it got my undivided attention!

"Don't you *ever* laugh at your father again," she rasped through clenched teeth, "or anybody *else* who is humiliated."

I wasn't sure what humiliated meant, but I knew for certain it wasn't something to laugh about.

Except for two words—*nanna* and *sleep*—he couldn't speak. I missed his laughter and boisterous singing, but the crippling illness put him on his back most of the time and the laughter was gone. My mother had the impossible task of being both mother and father to me and my two sisters.

I never saw her cry or get angry, although she must have done both when nobody else was around. In spite of our poverty, with three small children to raise and a severely disabled husband to care for, her courage and confidence seemed like something chiseled out of stone—sturdy and unshakeable. I never knew we were poor until I was much older.

* * *

My father's life was a brutal study in frustration.

Many times I saw him boil over in exasperation when he couldn't communicate something simple to my mother. "Nanna! Sleep!" he would scream, waving his right fist in the air, obviously confused about what he heard himself saying and what his mind was trying to speak. Other times, he simply slumped back in his chair, shaking his head from side to side like a great wounded animal, as though to clear his muddled thinking. And then silent tears of despair rolled down his gaunt face.

There is something terrifying about watching a strong man cry silently.

The bewilderment and frustration of his existence finally exploded in violence. After repeated attempts at communicating something to my mother, his fist shot out, striking her solidly on the left side of her face. Even as her head snapped back from the blow, she stepped in close and tried to control his rage. Twice again I heard the dull smack of hard knuckles smashing into soft skin as she became the focal point of everything empty and debilitating about his life. While blood flowed freely from her lacerated mouth, she continued speaking calmly: "Erwin! Erwin, listen to me! Calm down! Control yourself!"

In the center of this powerful emotional storm, the young woman remained calm and focused. She wasn't afraid of being hurt—her fear was that he would suffer another stroke.

Moments later, slumped again in his chair, with his face twisted in confusion and the rage spent like air from a lanced balloon, the silent tears again ran down his face.

Both parents were oblivious to my presence. My mother quickly went about the business of repairing the damage to her face, washing away the blood and applying an ice pack to her swollen mouth, while discreetly watching my father carefully for any sign of injury to himself. A woman who wouldn't have tolerated physical violence from a man for one second under different circumstances, intuitively knew my father wasn't entirely responsible for his behavior and she wasn't distracted by anger or bitterness.

The tears passed and he sat quietly in his chair, looking curiously at his useless left hand, picking it up with his right and letting it drop back in his lap like something dead. He kept staring at his hand as though it was a foreign appendage, a strange and distasteful part of himself that he no longer recognized.

Later that day, my Uncle Merlin, Dad's older brother, came to the house. After one look at my mother's battered, swollen, and discolored face, he glared at my father and then exploded himself.

"Jean, this man is dangerous and it's time you faced that fact!" he roared. "Look at your face. Look at your face! He's going to accidentally kill you one of these days. Do you want your kids to see that? You're gonna have to put him in a state institution for his own good."

Her weary and bruised face tightened, suddenly flushed with deeply felt anger. As though shrugging off the fatigue she felt, she slowly stood up and faced my uncle. Her voice remained calm and steady, but the words shot out of her mouth like the steady fire of a jackhammer.

"When I married Erwin, the vows were for 'better or worse.' And it can't get much worse than now," she said, looking at my father slumped in his chair, his face telegraphing great shame and defeat.

"But I will *never* have my husband locked up in any

institution as long as I can take care of him myself, and you will never bring that subject up again," she shouted. "I will *never* leave him or abandon him. Do you understand that? *Never!*" she hissed through bloody lips.

For the next five years she struggled with the demanding task of raising three small children, caring for my father, and working at any odd job she could find in order to make enough money for our needs. As his health slowly deteriorated, leaving him helpless, speechless, and bedridden, she continued treating him with dignity and respect until the day he died.

I never gave any thought about what motivated her behavior toward my father when I was a child. When I began thinking about such issues in academy and college, I thought she simply did her duty like she was supposed to do. Later, I realized her motives were both simple and profound: she loved him, and her behavior toward him reflected that love, a love deeply rooted in her religious convictions. It was a concrete reflection of her faith in action.

More than 30 years have come and gone since then. What I observed in my home as a child taught me some powerful lessons about values when I too faced some adversity in my own life. Without ever speaking in theological terms, my mother taught me about loyalty, duty, compassion, forgiveness, tenacity, human dignity, and calm restraint when confronted with the most savage provocation. In short, my mother *lived* God's grace.

"Hello in there!" Valerie said, interrupting my distant thoughts. "Did you forget my question?"

I backed away from those old memories, feeling curiously refreshed, and looked at her warm smile.

"No, I didn't forget your question. But let me answer it by telling you a story about some very costly grace."